Comp. 5

Frederic DeSautoy.

Bought of Lumley 126. A. Holten

AN ESSAY

ON

SYMBOLIC COLOURS,

IN ANTIQUITY—THE MIDDLE AGES—AND MODERN TIMES.

FROM THE FRENCH OF "LE BARON FRÉDÉRIC DE PORTAL,

MAITRE DES REQUÉTES, CHEVALIER DE LA LEGION D'HONNEUR.

WITH NOTES,

By W. S. INMAN, Arch.; Assoc. Inst. Civil Engineers.

IN THREE SECTIONS.

WITH ILLUSTRATIVE ENGRAVINGS.

LONDON:

JOHN WEALE, 59, HIGH HOLBORN.

MDCCCXLV.

LONDON:

GEORGE WOODFALL AND SON,

ANGEL COURT, SKINNER STREET.

PREFACE.

THIS Essay was originally translated for Mr. Weale's Quarterly Papers on Architecture; each section has a title, which, in a *separate* publication, may appear superfluously repeated, but after the limited number for the periodical was printed, the Essay seemed so generally illustrative of the archæology of art, that an addition of one hundred in number of impressions was desired for publication in a separate form.

ED.

April 1, 1845.

SYMBOLIC COLOURS.

INTRODUCTION.

" SYMBOLISM in all art is a great excellence, perhaps its essence." This reannounce-ment in the present prevalence of mechanical opinions may be cavilled at; but every thing tending to promote sound principles is worthy of public attention. The eminent critic's sentiment evinces a mind imbued not only with the love, but with the know-ledge of the Utility of the Fine Arts. The Polychromy of architecture has been too much neglected : it will be found coeval with specimens of the highest antiquity.

At a period when the ancient palace of the Kings of England, rebuilding for Par-liament, is to be decorated with paintings under the sanction of Commissioners of acknowledged taste, and the presidency of THE PRINCE CONSORT of the realm; when Ecclesiastical rites and ceremonies are reviving, and the appropriate insignia of churches generally discussed, it seems a fit opportunity for publishing an Essay on Symbolic Colours, which are so closely connected with these interesting subjects.

In remote antiquity, before the use of letters; in the middle ages, during the decline of literature,—and long afterward from its slow revival; colours were evi-dence of traditions, the written language of the people; the "signs of the times." In ancient Egypt the same hieroglyphic, in ancient Greece the same word, was synonymous for writing and painting. We have been so accustomed to consider as *real*, what is truly *symbolic*, that we unconsciously transfer the one for the other, the representative for the thing signified. *Words* are but *symbols* of our ideas by the medium of sound; and all nations (however their languages may differ) use symbolic characters or figures in arithmetic, music, astronomy, &c. No two sciences could ap-parently have less natural relation to figures than colours and music; yet the har-monies of both are based on certain numbers in accurate proportion, a deviation from

which is destructive to beauty in either. Black and white are but the result of absorption and reflexion of the three primary colours in a fixed ratio.

The theory of the Symbolism of Colours in the following Essay may be traced
to its origin in the annals of Creation. The creation of Light[*] was anterior to that
of Colour. The Sun is the natural source of Colour; the theory, therefore, is not
incompatible with the original symbols attributed to it—the Sun, the great vivifier
of Nature—typified in Mythology, the Divine Author of Eternal Life. Hence the
Memphite *Phrè*, the Theban and Grecian *Pire*—" the Sons of the Sun"; the Pharaohs of Egypt: are brethren of the Virgins of the Sun; the Priestesses of Peru.

The indications of Colour are significant and important in the Sacred Scriptures, in Mythology, in Heraldry, in Architecture, in Fleets and Armies. They
explain much of the origin and analogy of languages and customs, proving them to be
symbolic and phonetic. We are still required to "sign" (not write) our names, and
a seal is essential to the legal validity of every "deed." They tend to elucidate the
apparent obscurity of Sabean worship, of Egyptian and Chinese hieroglyphics, of
the Orphic and Eleusinian mysteries; of ancient and modern art, in costume,
stained glass, gems, &c., of the Quipos of the South, and the Wampum of the North
American—symbols extending to our own days, and, like the colour of the aborigines,
connecting the past and the present, the Old World and the New, the Red Indian
with the progenitor of mankind [אדם Adam—the *Red* Man].

In the public solemnities of coronations, installations, baptisms, marriages, and
burials, the prevailing colours evince the *animus* of joy and sorrow, the purity and
fidelity, of those engaged. The Colours of Armies are their Dii Penates; they are
still consecrated by the priest, and honoured and saluted by sovereigns and soldiers.
The Theologist's objection of tendency to Materialism applies to every *visible*
representation, but obviously arises from the abuse rather than the use of religious
emblems, which may be obviated by a knowledge of the true expressions and application of Colours. The more antiquarian researches are extended, the more con-
firmatory are they of Scripture History. The colours and precious stones in the
Hebrew high priest's vestments and breast-plate, symbolize the utmost perfection of
Purity, Wisdom and Justice, Truth and Virtue.

Men of philosophical minds will admit that a medium (abstractedly considered)
having no form, substance, or dimension, but forming harmonic triads, and so evanescent as almost to defy definition, might not inappropriately represent to a primitive
people the immateriality of the Supreme—if all and every such representation were

---

[*] Probably electric light and fire originating basaltic, granitic, metallic, and other formations.

not divinely prohibited ;—but the last act of creation, the visible token of the covenant with man, by his beneficent Saviour from the Deluge, was ratified by colours :—but who ever worshipped the rainbow ? And yet is there any one who can regard it without humble gratitude to God for this symbol of safety and subsistence, " from generation to generation"? To the sceptic's objection, that its appearance is the effect of natural causes of sunshine and rain—there are good answers: but he must preliminarily prove their previous coexistence ; the second chapter of Genesis, 5th and 6th verses, and the 4th of the seventh chapter imply the contrary, and that the rain of waters must have been as terrific a judgment to the Old World as the subsequent rain of fire was to the New.

True knowledge of the use and abuse of symbols, will also tend to increased caution in their use in ecclesiastical edifices, rites, and ceremonies, and to prevent the misinterpretation of those sanctioned " by authority," and the introduction of others without such sanction : that " all things be done in order."

To the objection of the sinister or double meaning of colours, many phrases are equally obnoxious ; e. g. the French word " sacre ;" the English word " rank ;" in ancient Egypt, " Pharaoh, son of a Pharaoh," the highest of personal descent ; and in modern Egypt the most opprobrious of contempt.

The following Essay assumes not a scientific form ; it states various applications of the subject, referring to authorities for the accuracy of its examples. The translator will be happy if he thus make more generally known the researches of so distinguished a savant as M. Frédéric Portal, on a subject from which, for some years past, he himself has derived much pleasure and instruction.

SYMBOLIC COLOURS,

IN ANTIQUITY—THE MIDDLE AGES—AND MODERN TIMES.

FROM THE FRENCH OF FREDERIC PORTAL.

WITH NOTES.

By W. S. INMAN, Assoc.Inst. Civil Engineers.

The history of symbolic colours, as yet but little known, and of which I present only fragments, will, perhaps, tend to decipher the hieroglyphics of Egypt, and to unveil some of the mysteries of antiquity. I do not flatter myself that I have accomplished the object of my investigations: my sole ambition is to excite the attention of the learned on one of the most curious and neglected points of archæology.

Colours had the same signification amongst all nations of remotest antiquity; this conformity indicates a common origin, which extends to the earliest state of humanity, and developes its highest energies in the religion of Persia; the dualism of light and darkness presents, in effect, the two types of colours which become the symbols of two principles, benevolence and malevolence. The ancients admitted but two primitive colours, white and black, whence all others were derived; the divinities of Paganism were likewise emanations of the good and evil principle.

The language of colours, intimately connected with religion, passed into India, China, Egypt, Greece, Rome, reappeared in the middle ages, and the large windows of Gothic cathedrals found their explanation in the books of the Zends, the Vedas, and the paintings of Egyptian temples.

The identity of symbols implies the identity of primitive creeds; but in proportion as religion departs from its principle, degrades and materializes itself, she forsakes the signification of colours; and this mysterious language revives with religious truth. The nearer the origin of religions is approximated, the more truth appears despoiled of the impure alloy of human superstitions; she shines with the most vivid light in Iran, the country of the most ancient people. According to Mohsen Fany, "the Iranians believed firmly, that a Supreme God created the world by an act of his power, and that his providence governed it continually; they profess to fear him, to love him, to piously adore him, to honour their relations and aged persons; they had a fraternal affection for all mankind, and even a tender compassion for animals."[a]

The worship of the heavenly host, Sabeism, obscured these sublime doctrines, without annihilating them; they were preserved in the Desatir and Zent-Avesta; and if the truth were hidden from the profane, it was yet discoverable under the symbols of these sacred books.

The more a religion advances from its origin, the more it materializes itself; from degradation to degradation, it arrives at Fetism; the adoration of the Negroes is the last expression of the dogmas of Ethiopia and Egypt[b]. Already in the time of Moses, the Egyptian religion evinced the elements of decrepitude and dissolution; the symbol was become the god: truth, forgotten by the people, was exiled from the sanctuaries; and very soon the priests themselves began to lose the signification of their sacred language; these observations equally apply to India and its corrupt Brahmins, to China and its shameful Bonzes, to those Israelites who sacrificed to the idols of foreigners; and to every mode of worship.

This custom, fatal to humanity, explains the necessity of successive revelations; Judaism and Christianity are divine, by the isolated fact that the intervention of the Divinity was necessary, indispensable. How otherwise can the progress of mankind in spiritual religion be reconciled with the tendency of every people to materialize its worship?

The antique religion of Iran is forgotten; its sacred *symbols*, the light, the sun, the planets, are deified. It is at the epoch when this revolution is accomplished; that Abraham goes out of Chaldea; and revivifies the truth, about to be annihilated. In Egypt and India the priesthood still preserved the depositories of sacred knowledge, but the people were immersed in ignorance. Polytheism shrouded the world with its funereal veil; and then God revealed himself in the call of the patriarch, and from one family, as the element of society, religion was propagated in the world.

This prevailing human tendency led to the idolatry of the captive Jews in Egypt.

---

[a] Dabistan et les Recherches Asiatiques, traduction, tom. ii. p. 98.

[b] The gods of the Egyptians, the Phenicians, the Canaanites, &c., like those of the Negroes, were small idols, called Ptha, Phethic, Phateig, whence the Greeks derived the name (Φατις) Phatis, and which, preserved unaltered amongst the Negroes, is exactly their word Fetish or Fetich.—Cours de Gebelin, Monde primitif, tom. viii.

Moses appeared, the truth was demonstrated, and the elect people, scarcely snatched from vain superstitions, relapsed into lethargy. In the desert they sacrificed to the calf Apis; they trampled under foot the holy law in the land of Israel, separated themselves, and invoked the bloody gods of the barbarians. But the Eternal will not abandon the work of regeneration; the prophet nation had accomplished its mission, and the Son of God, the Saviour of the world, appeared in his humanity to call all nations to the feast of life.

Thus the fall of the first man is reflected in the history of every people. This fatal consequence establishes the universal doctrine of the forfeiture and reinstatement by divine intervention.

The first chapters of Genesis enshrine this truth, and the voice of the prophets proclaimed it in Israel; but it is not the Hebrew nation only which raise their hopes and prayers to the Eternal; Persia, India, China, Greece, Rome, expect the Saviour of the world. Call me not the Holy, said Confucius to his disciples; the Holy is in the West; and it is from the East the Magi departed, and those envoys of the Emperor Ming-Ti, who brought back from India the worship of the god Fo[a]. But Volney and Dupuis mention these oriental traditions, and attribute them to the worship of the sun, doubtless forgetting that this star rose in the East, and that the Holy One should appear in the West.

The incarnation of the Indian divinity was borrowed from Christianity, I admit; but if it be true, as science authorizes, that the sacred books of India be anterior to our æra, would not the mystery of Krichna be the most astonishing of prophecies?

Egypt claims the same dogmas, and engraved them on the Temples of Thebes, Orpheus repeated them in Greece, and the sybilline verses announced them to the queen of the world. If I were to repeat portions of these prophetic songs, some Christians would say that they were fabricated or falsified; but were the verses of Virgil inspired by a Gothic monk? Or would the pagan Servius, who comments on them, be a critic of the convent?[b]

If Virgil were a Roman, if he flourished in the time of Augustus, how did he announce that the last times predicted by the sybil are accomplished? that the golden age advances, that the sun, eternal symbol of the divine world, expands its light? What is this virgin, this child, which should change the face of the world? It is Augustus, reply the learned commentators; but if the flattery of the poet applies this prediction to a man, does he not address it to a God?

[a] Mémoires concernant les Chinois, tom. v. p. 59.

[b] The Jesuit Hardouin pretended that the Æneid of Virgil was fabricated by monks in the cloisters of Citeaux, it was doubtless a joke or mystification.

The gross mob of antiquity adored the material symbols of a worship divine in its origin; the school of the eighteenth century would see the adoration of the sun in Christianity; every religion is born in spirituality, and quenches itself in materialism. The incredulous fetichism of Dupuis, as the superstitious fetichism of antiquity, denounces the destruction of a church, and demands a new religious regeneration.

Truth appears strange to humanity: a gift from heaven, men repudiate or pervert it. The principle of paganism should be sought in the human heart, and not in history, which can only apprehend its exterior manifestation. Policy has not given birth to idolatry; she knows how to profit by it, to give it new powers, but not to create that infinite variety of divinities. The unity of God would doubtless have been the religion created by oriental despotism; the unity of the government proclaims it. Polytheism would only produce schisms and divisions.

The symbols of the Divinity, materialized by important nations, were the origin of creeds which besotted the people of antiquity, and arrested, for four thousand years, the march of the human intellect.

St. Clement of Alexandria informs us that the Egyptians used three sorts of characters for writing[a]. Varro, the most learned Roman, establishes the existence of three theologies; and we find, in the history of religions, three epochs, marked by three distinct languages.

The *Divine Language* at first addresses itself to all men, and reveals to them the existence of God. Symbolism is the language of every people, as religion is the property of each family; the priest as yet exists not, each father is king and pontiff.

The *Consecrated Language* commenced in the sanctuaries, it regulates the symbolism of Architecture, of Sculpture and of Painting, as well as the ceremonies of worship and the costume of priests; this primary materialization confines the divine language under impenetrable veils.

The *Profane Language*, the material expression of symbols, is the provision assigned, to nations given up to idolatry.

At first God speaks to man the heavenly language contained in the Bible and the most ancient religious codes of the East; but soon the sons of Adam forget this heritage, and God reiterates the word under the symbols of the consecrated language. It regulates the costume of Aaron and of the Levites, and the rites of worship; religion becomes exterior; man wishes to see it; he no more feels it within him.

In the last degree of corruption humanity only comprehends the material; accord-

---

[a] St. Clement, Bishop of Alexandria, A.D. 194, in his "Stromates," says, "Those who, among the Egyptians, receive instruction, learn first, that species of writing which is termed *epistolographic* (the popular); they next learn the *hieratic* (sacerdotal); and lastly, the *hieroglyphic* (or sacred).

ingly, the divine word becomes incarnate to make it heard in the profane language as a last echo of eternal truth [a].

The history of symbolic colours testifies this triple origin; each gradation of colour bears different significations in each of the three languages, Divine, Consecrated, and Profane.

Let us briefly follow the historical development of these symbols.

The most ancient religious traditions inform us that the Iranians assign to each planet a beneficent or malignant influence according to their colour and their degree of light.

In Genesis God says to Noah, The rainbow shall be the sign of the covenant between me and the earth. In Mythology, Iris is the messenger of the gods, and of good tidings; and the colours of the cincture of Iris, the rainbow, are the symbols of regeneration, which is the covenant of God and man.

In Egypt, the robe of Isis was resplendent with all colours, of every hue displayed in nature; Osiris the god all powerful, gives the light, Isis modifies it, and transmits it to man by reflection. Isis [b] is reflection, the earth and her symbolic robe was the hieroglyphic of the material and of the spiritual world.

The fathers of the church, those Platonics of Christianity, saw in the Old Testament the symbols of the new covenant; if the religion of Christ be of God, if the children of Abraham received the Holy Word, the two tables of the Mosaic and of Christian law, would unite in one common expression. Joseph was a symbol of the Messiah, and his robe diapered with the most beautiful tints, which his father gave him, was, says Saint Cyril, the emblem of his divine attributes.

Such were the symbols of divine language, when the *consecrated* language was instituted.

Religion gave birth to the Arts. It was to ornament temples and sacred precincts that sculpture and painting were first introduced: this fact is applicable not only to the history of the human race, but is found true in the origin of every people. In the most ancient monuments of India and Egypt, as in those of the middle ages, Architecture, Sculpture, and Painting are the material expressions of religious thoughts.

Painting among the Hindoos, the Egyptians, and still in our days amongst the

---

[a] Let us here note the way of God and that of man. In Iran pure idealism reigns; the ancient Persians, according to Herodotus, had no temples; in India dogmatic spiritualism appears; in Egypt human rationalism, and in Greece sensualism. Such is the retrograde march of the human mind. At length God, recommencing his denaturalized work, restores truth to man by the call of Abraham, by the mission of the Israelitish nation, and by Christianity; revealing himself at first to a single family, He soon instructs a nation to call mankind to Himself.

[b] Is-Is (or ish-ish, light-light), the shining forth. D. Morison, Religious History.

Chinese, imposes its regulations, in the national worship and politic laws; the least alteration in the drawing or colouring would incur a serious punishment.

Among the Egyptians, writes Synesius, the Prophets did not allow metal founders or statuaries to represent the gods, for fear that they should deviate from the rules.

" In the temples of Egypt," says Plato, " it was never allowed, nor is it permitted at this day, neither to painters, nor to any artists who make figures or other similar works, to innovate in any thing, nor to deviate in any way, from that which has been regulated by the laws of the country ; and if the subject be investigated, there would be found amongst them works of painting and sculpture made ten thousand years ago (when I say ten thousand years it is not literally speaking) which are neither more nor less beautiful than those of the present day, which have been wrought by the same rules." [a]

At Rome, the penalty of death was incurred by selling or being clothed in a purple stuff [b]. At this day, in China, any one who wears or buys clothes with the prohibited designs of the dragon or phœnix [c], incurs three hundred stripes, and three years' banishment [d].

Symbolism explains this severity of laws and customs; to each colour, to each pattern, appertained a religious or political idea; to change or to alter it was a crime of apostasy or of rebellion.

Archæologists have remarked that Indian and Egyptian paintings, and those of Greek origin named Etruscan, are composed of plain tints of a brilliant colour, but without demi-tints [e]; this is as it ought to be. Art did not speak only to the profane, it was still the interpreter and depository of sacred mysteries. The pattern and the colour had a necessary signification,—it was essentially restrictive; perspective, chiaro oscuro, and demi-tints, would have led to confusion; they were unknown, or their manifestation severely repressed.

We may affirm, without referring to any authority, that if the design of Egyptian hieroglyphics were symbolic, the colour was equally so : does it not, in effect, present the most direct means of affecting the spectator and attracting notice : even in our own days, are not great colourists more popular than great delineators?

Reverting to the origin of writing, colour evidently was the first mode of transmitting thought and preserving memory. The quipos of Peru and the Chinese

[a] The Laws of Plato, Book II.
[b] Justinian Code, Lib. 4. tit. 40.
[c] Phœnim, the faces, or cherubim ?
[d] Code Penal de la Chine, tom. ii. p. 340.
[e] Quatremère de Quincy de l'Architect. Égyptienne, p. 167.

strings tinted with various colours formed the archives, religious, political, and administrative, of these primitive people[a]. The Mexicans made one step further in the art of representing speech, and we shall perceive that colours perform an important part in the paintings of this nation: the Egyptian hieroglyphics were the apogee, and the last term of this symbolic writing.

The *profane language* of colours was a degradation from the divine and the consecrated languages. Traces reappear among the Greeks and Romans. In scenic representations the colours were significative. A curious passage of Pollux[b] explains these emblems employed in the costume of the theatre; tradition still finds them there, but materialized in our own times.

Christianity, in recalling these forgotten significations, restores a new energy to the language of colours; the doctrine taught by Christ was not therefore new, since it borrowed the symbols of ancient religions. The Son of God, in leading back mankind to the truth, came not to change but to fulfil the law; this law was the worship of the true God, revealed primitively to all men, and preserved in the holy ark of Judaism; Moses and the prophets quote some sacred books which are not found in the Bible; the wars of the Lord, the prophecies and the book of the Just[c] had then announced the Divine word to other nations. We shall find manifest proof of this in investigating the monuments of antiquity and of the middle ages.

The three languages of colours—divine, consecrated, and profane—classify, in Europe, the three estates of society—the clergy, the nobles, and the people.

The large glass windows of Christian churches, like the paintings of Egypt, have a double signification, the apparent and the hidden; the one is for the uninitiated, the other applies itself to the mystic creeds. The theocratic era lasts to the renaissance; at this epoch symbolic expression is extinct; the divine language of colours is forgotten, painting becomes an art, and is no longer a science[d].

The aristocratic era commences; symbolism banished from the church, takes refuge at the court; disdained by painting, it is found again in heraldry.

The origin of armorial bearings loses itself in the dark ages, and appears connected with the first elements of writing; Egyptian hieroglyphics, like the earliest

---

[a] Vide Garcillaso de la Vega—History of the Incas and of Chou-Kong.

[b] Julii Pollucis Onomasticum, lib. iv. cap. 18.

[c] Vide Numbers xxi., Jeremiah xlviii., 2 Kings, chap. i., Joshua x., 1 Kings, chap. xi. v. 41. Compare the Preliminary Discourse of Bhaguat-Geeta, p. 15.

[d] In pictures of the middle ages, the more the influence of art is perceptible, the less are traces of symbolism discoverable. The bible of the 10th century, preserved in the " Bibliothèque Royale ". is one of the most curious monuments of symbolism, and one of the most pitiable for the drawing.

Aztic paintings, indicate the signification of a subject by emblems or speaking arms; it is sufficient to glance over the Mexican paintings, and the explanation which has been preserved to us, to remove any doubt in this respect [a]. The representations of Indian and Egyptian divinities, compounded of monstrous human and animal forms, had doubtless a hidden meaning; in Greece, the progress of art liberated sculpture and painting from these hybrid creations, but the divinities were confounded in a similar type. Attributes were given them; Jupiter had for arms, the eagle and the thunderbolt; Minerva, the olive and the owl; Venus, the dove.

The middle ages renewed the strange creations of remote antiquity; mixed compositions appear on the most ancient monuments of Christian art; Christianity, like Paganism, could not sculpture and paint its dogmas, except by borrowing symbolical language; it is thus that the Queen Pedauque was represented with the foot of a goose on the portal of several churches in France [b].

The emblazoned shields of the nobles were barred with iron, as the only mode of recognising the knights in the mêlée. In their origin all arms were significant: the kingdom of Grenada had nine grenades; that of Galicia a chalice; that of Leon a lion; and that of Castile a castle [c]. Afterwards heraldry perpetuated in families the memory of great actions and high deeds of arms; but the primitive signification was more frequently forgotten.

Colours were doubtless significative in these representations, where all was emblematic. Authors of the heraldic art affirm it, and we have preserved the meaning of metals and enamels, of which the tradition extends to the Greeks [d].

I shall explain the symbolism of these different colours of heraldry: the traditions of antiquity preserved them pure for a long period, and on some monuments the solemn language of arms facilitates the apprehension of the Divine language employed in the principal subject, as phonetic writing inclosed in a cartouche, gives the name of the personage represented on Egyptian anaglyphs.

The gallantry of the Moors, and their amorous mysticism, closed the aristocratic

[a] Recueil de Thévenot.
[b] Bullet, Mythologie Française, p. 33.
[c] Pasquier, p. 142.
[d] All coats of arms, says Anselme, in the Palais de l'Honneur, are differenced by two metals, five colours, and two furs. The two metals are or (gold), and argent (silver); the five colours are azure, gueules (red), sable (black), sinople (green), and pourpre (violet); the two skins or furs are ermine and vair. Aristotle in his time gave names to metals and colours according to the seven planets. Or, was called the Sun; argent, the Moon; azure, Jupiter; gueules, Mars; sable, Saturn; sinople, Venus; and pourpre, Mercury; and each god was invested and painted with his appropriate metal and colour. (Comp. Court de Gebelin, Monde primitif, tom. viii. p. 200.)

era; and introduced the popular language of colours, which is preserved to our times.

The seclusion of females in the east, gave a new importance to the emblems of colours; they replaced the colloquial language, as the selam or symbolic bouquet became the written language of love.

Among the Arabs, as amongst all nations, this language had a religious origin. In ancient Persia, the spirits or genii had flowers which were consecrated to them [a]. This symbolic Flora is found in India and in Egypt, in Greece and at Rome [b].

The Selam of the Arabs appears to have borrowed its emblems from the language of colours; the Koran gives the mystic reason. The colours that the earth exhibits to our eyes, says Mahomet, are manifest signs for those who think [c]. This remarkable passage explains the diapered robe borne by Isis or Nature conceived as a vast hieroglyphic. The colours which shine on the earth correspond to the shadows which the seer perceives in the world of spirits, where all is spiritual and consequently significative. Such, at least, is the origin of the symbolism of colours in the books of Prophecy and the Apocalypse. The Koran reproduces the same theory in the visions and costumes of Mahomet.

The Moors of Spain, materializing these symbols, formed a language, which had its principles and its dictionary. A modern author has given a catalogue of more than sixty of these emblematic colours, their meaning and their combinations [d]. France has adopted them, and preserves their traces in popular language. Blue is still the emblem of fidelity, yellow of jealousy, red of cruelty, white of innocence, black of sadness and mourning, and green of hope.

Thus ends the symbolism of colours, and however its last expression may be materialized, it yet testifies its noble origin. Modern painting still preserves its traditions in church pictures: St. John wears a green robe, Christ and the Virgin are likewise draped in red and blue, and God in white. Symbolism, that antique science, became an art, and is at present little more than an affair of the workshop.

---

[a] Boun-Dehesch, p. 407.

[b] A learned German intends to publish the mythological history of flowers in Greece and Rome. [Dierbach, Flora mythologica, oder Pfauzenkunde in bezug auf Mythologie und Symbolik der Griechen und Romer.] We shall establish the existence of these traditions in the middle ages, their last popular expression is preserved in our own, and the author of the language of flowers has collected the emblematic signification of 190 plants. Delachenaye's Alphabet of Flora, or Language of Flowers, P. Didot, l'aîné, 1811.

[c] Koran, chap. 16 les Abeilles, trad. de Savary.

[d] Gassier, Histoire de la Chevalerie Française, p. 351, &c.

PRINCIPLES OF THE SYMBOLISM OF COLOURS.

Previous to reestablishing the catalogue of symbolic colours, it is requisite to learn the grammatical rules of the language. Proceeding by analysis in the course of these researches, it would, perhaps, be difficult to comprehend the generation of symbols, if the synthesis, which governs the system, did not precede them.

Natural philosophy recognises seven colours, which form the solar ray, decomposed by the prism, namely, violet, indigo, blue, green, yellow, orange, and red.

Painting admits but five primitives, the first and last of which are rejected by natural philosophy, namely, white, yellow, red, blue, and black. From the combination of these five colours every hue is produced.

According to symbolism, two principles produce all colours, light and darkness.

Light is represented by white, and darkness by black; but light does not exist but by fire, the symbol of which is red. Setting out from this basis, symbolism admits two primitive colours, red, and white*. Black was considered as the negation of colours, and attributed to the spirit of darkness; red is the symbol of divine love; white the symbol of divine wisdom. From these two attributes of God, love and wisdom, the creation of the universe emanates.

Secondary colours represent different combinations of the two principles.

Yellow emanates from red and white, it is the symbol of the revelation of the love and of the wisdom of God*.

Blue emanates likewise from red and white; it indicates divine wisdom manifested by life, by the Spirit or the breath of God [air, azure], it is the symbol of the Spirit of Truth. St. John, xiv. 17, and xvi. 13.

Green is formed by the union of yellow and blue, it indicates the manifestation of love and wisdom in action; it was the symbol of charity, and of the regeneration of the soul by works.

In this system three degrees are recognised:

    1. Existence in itself.
    2. Manifestation of life.
    3. The act which results.

In the first degree love rules the desire or the will, marked by the red and the white; in the second appears intelligence, speech or the word, designated by yellow and

---

* Symbolism is not to be understood as declaring that yellow may be composed of red and of white, because these form the rose; but the symbol of yellow emanates from the symbol of red, and from the symbol of white; thus divine revelation, indicated by yellow, emanates from divine love and divine wisdom, designated by red and white.

blue; and in the third, the realization, or the act, finds its symbol in the green colour. These three degrees, which recall the three operations of the human understanding, the will, the judgment, and the act, are also found in every colour. Three significations are to be noted according to the greater or less degree of light; thus the same tint indicates three orders of ideas, accordingly as it may appear in the luminous ray that it colours, secondly in the translucid body, and lastly in the opaque.

Painting could not reproduce these differences which we establish in the written monuments of antiquity. The vestments of God shine like lightning, as a flame of fire, as a ray of the sun; it is the coloured light which reveals to the prophet the love and the will of the Divinity.

Precious stones, transparent, formed the second degree indicated by the light reflected interiorly; they related to the interior of man or to the spiritual world; at last opaque bodies, as stones, vestments of linen, which project the light from their surface, indicate the third degree, or the natural, which is manifested in the act.

We shall occupy ourselves but little with these differences. It is, however, necessary to indicate them, in order to apprehend the absolute value of symbols. White, for example, signifies wisdom in three degrees; but, in the first, the white light will denote divine wisdom, which is goodness itself; in the second degree, the diamond and the crystal will be the symbols of spiritual wisdom, which possesses the interior intellect of the Divinity; and lastly, in the third degree, the white and opaque stone, and the vestments of linen, will signify natural wisdom, or external faith, which produces works.

RULE OF COMBINATIONS.

After the five colours, come the compound hues; rose, purple, hyacinth, violet, grey, tan, &c. These hues receive their significations from the colours which compose them. That which predominates, gives to the hue its general signification, and that which is subordinate, the modified. Thus, purple, which is of a red azure, signifies the love of truth; and hyacinth, which is of a blue purple, represents the truth of love. These two significations would seem to confound themselves at their source, but the applications will show the difference which exists between them.

RULE OF OPPOSITIONS.

The rule of oppositions is common to the language of colours, and to all symbols in general. It attributes to them the signification opposed to that which they possess directly. In Genesis, the serpent represents the evil genius, and the fathers of the church call the Messiah the good serpent. In Egypt, water was the symbol of regeneration, and the sea was consecrated to Typhon, the type of moral degradation. Thus, red signifies love, egotism, and hatred; green, celestial regeneration and infernal degradation, wisdom, and folly. This rule, far from causing obscurity or arbitrariness in the signification of symbols, gives them an energy unknown to common expressions.

The symbolism of colours would excel by this mode, and has preserved it as one of its greatest beauties. In effect, black, united to other colours, gives them the contrary signification. The symbol of evil and falsehood, black, is not a colour, but the negation of all hues, and of that which they represent. Thus, red will designate divine love; united with black, it will be the symbol of infernal love, of egotism, of hatred, and of all the passions of degraded man.

In the preceding pages, I believe that I have satisfactorily established that colours were symbolic in antiquity and the middle ages. In the following I shall investigate this signification from historical and religious sources. I hope to demonstrate, that if colours were significative, they did represent the ideas that I assign to them.

OF WHITE.

DIVINE LANGUAGE.

God is life, the unity which embraces the universe. I am that I am, said Jehovah. The white colour should be the symbol of absolute truth, of Him who is. It alone reflects all the luminous rays; it is the unity whence emanate the primitive colours, and the thousand hues which colour nature.

Wisdom, said Solomon, is the emanation radiating from the Divine Almighty, the purity of eternal light, the spotless mirror of the works of God, and the image of his goodness; and, being but one, can do all things [a].

The prophets saw the Divinity clothed with a mantle white as snow, and his hair white, or compared to pure wool [b]. God created the universe in his love, and ordered it by his wisdom. In all cosmogonies, divine wisdom, eternal light, subdues primitive darkness, and makes the world issue from the bosom of chaos.

[a] Liber Sapientiæ, cap. vii. 25.   [b] Daniel, cap. vii. et x.

In the beginning, (Genesis,) God created the heaven and the earth; the earth was without form, and void; darkness remained on the abyss, and the Spirit of God hovered on the waters.

According to an oracle cited by St. Justin and Eusebius, the Chaldeans had the same doctrine as the Hebrews respecting the divinity[a]. They called fire a principle, fire intellect, splendour uncreated, eternal, figurative expressions, equally consecrated by the biblical books. Jehovah appeared in a burning bush,—a luminous column conducted the children of Israel in the desert. The sacred fire of the tabernacle is the symbol of the presence of God in Israel,—his throne is the sun.

Genesis assigns to light and to darkness a separate empire[b]. The ancient Persians attached every idea of the good and the beautiful to the first principle, and of evil and disorder to the second.

This dualism is found again in every religion, according to an observation of Plutarch[c], confirmed by the discoveries of science. The Persians named the one Ormusd and the other Ahriman.

"Ormusd, says the Zent-Avesta, is raised above all. He was with sovereign knowledge, with purity in the light of the world. This throne of light,—this place inhabited by Ormusd, is that which is called primitive light. Ahriman was in the darkness with his law, and the dark place which he inhabited is that which is called primitive darkness. He was alone in the midst of them,—he who is called the wicked."[d]

These two principles, isolated in the bosom of the boundless abyss, unite themselves, create the world, and thence their powers received limits.

The laws of Manou taught the Indians that the world was plunged in obscurity: then the Lord, self-existing, shining with the purest brightness, appeared and dissipated the obscurity[e].

The Pimander, a work which reproduces the Egyptian doctrine, whoever may be its editor, establishes the same dogma; the light appears, it disperses the darknesses which change into the humid principle[f]. In the traditions preserved by the Greeks, Osiris is the luminous god: his name, according to Plutarch, signifies him who has many eyes: his head is ornamented with sparkling bands, shadowless, without mix-

[a] Par. ad gent. et demonstr. evang. 3: compare Batteux, causes premières, p. 29.
[b] Divisit lucem et tenebras.
[c] Treatise on Isis and Osiris.
[d] Boun-dehesch, pp. 343, 344.
[e] Lois de Manou, liv. i. sect. 5 et 6: compare Sir W. Jones's works, vol. iii. p. 352.
[f] Pimander, sect. iv.

ture of colours. Typhon is the spirit of darkness, identical with the Ahriman of the Persians.

Virgil, who had been initiated in the mysteries, and who has retraced their history in his description of hell, relates, after the Greeks, that the god Pan, white as snow, seduced the moon[a].

Pan was the universal fecundating principle of nature: his name, his colour, and goatish body, evidently indicated it; the moon was the symbol of the female principle, of the subject which received and reflected life, as the moon reflects the rays of the sun. Isis, among the Egyptians, was the lunar divinity, and the personification of the primitive waters, of night, and of chaos.

Grecian mythology arose on this general base, and produced all its force in the mythes of Jupiter and Pluto. John the Lybian attributes white colour to Jupiter, father of gods and men, whilst Pluto is the god of the dark abode,—the Ahriman of Greece.

The Romans adopted the same creeds, and the first day of January the consul, clothed in a white robe, ascended the capitol on a white horse, to celebrate the triumph of Jupiter, god of light, over the giants, the spirits of darknesses[b].

Oriental traditions, transmitted to Egypt, to Greece and Rome, extended into the north of Asia, invaded Europe, passed into America, and reappear on the monuments of Mexico.

In Thibet, as in India and Java, certain symbolic names are employed with the value of numbers; the language of colours offers the mystic reasons.

In the Thibetian language, *hot-tkar* signifies, in its proper sense, white light, and in a symbolic sense, designates unity: in India, *Tchandra* signifies the moon, and relates to the number 1, doubtless because of the white lustre of this star, symbol of divine wisdom[c].

China adopts the doctrine of Persia, of the combat of the good and evil genius, of light and darkness, or of heat and cold, and reproduces it under the names of perfect and imperfect matter[d].

The Scandinavians revived this doctrine in the Eddas: "In the beginning there was neither heaven, nor earth, nor waters, but the open abyss; to the north of the

[a] Georg. lib. iii. verse 391.

[b] Creuzer. Religions de l'antiquité, liv. vi. p. 796.

[c] Vide Asiatic Journal, July 1835, pp. 15, 16.

[d] Le Yu et le Yang, d'après les Savans, sont l'Ormusd et l'Ahriman des Livres Zends.-Visdelou. Notice sur l'Y-King, à la suite de Chou-King, p. 411–413 et 428.—Paultier. Mémoire sur la doctrine du Tao, p. 1–31 et 37.

abyss was the world of darkness, and to the south the world of fire."[a] Thus eternal truth is inscribed in the sacred codes of all people; God alone possesses self-existence, the world emanates by his purpose. White colour was at first the symbol of divine unity; later, it designated the good principle struggling against the evil; it appertained to Christianity to re-establish the dogma and its symbol in their primitive purity; and when in the transfiguration the countenance of Jesus became brilliant as the sun, and his vesture white as snow[b], the apostles saw the Divinity itself, Jehovah, appear in the Son of God.

CONSECRATED LANGUAGE.

The priest represents the Divinity on earth. In all religions, the sovereign pontiff had white vestments, symbol of uncreated light.

Jehovah ordered Aaron not to enter the sanctuary unless clothed in white. Speak to Aaron, thy brother, said he, to Moses, that he enter not into the sanctuary at all times, lest he die; for I will reveal myself on the mercy-seat; he shall be invested with the holy linen robe, girt with the linen cincture, and he shall wear the mitre of linen; these are holy vestments[c].

The magi wore a white robe; they pretended that the Divinity was not pleased but with white robes. White horses were sacrificed to the sun, the image of divine light[d]. The white tunic given by Ormusd, the luminous god, is still the characteristic costume of the Parsees[e].

In Egypt a white tiara decorates the head of Osiris; his ornaments are white as those of Aaron, and the Egyptian priests wear the linen robe like the children of Levi[f]. In Greece, Pythagoras ordered the sacred hymns to be chaunted in white robes. The priests of Jupiter had white vestments. At Rome, the flamen dialis alone had the right to wear a white tiara; the victims offered to Jupiter are white[g]. Plato and Cicero consecrate this colour to the Divinity.

[a] Ampère Littérature et Voyages, p. 394. Finnæ Magnusen borealism. Myth. lexicon. Edda Antiquior, p. 17, and the Edda of Mallet.

[b] St. Matthew, chap. xvii. 2.

[c] Leviticus, chap. xvi. Compare Cunæus respub. Hebræor. lib. ii. cap. i.

[d] Diog. Laert. lib. i. p. 12. Brisson de Regno Persarum, lib. ii. initio. Pierii Hieroglyph. lib. xl. cap. xxii.

[e] Anquetil. Zent-Avesta, tom. ii. p. 529.

[f] Apuleii Metamorph. lib. xi. Herodoti, lib. ii. 37.

[g] Auli Gellii Noctes Atticæ, lib. x. cap. xv.

Returning into Asia, the same symbol is adopted by the Brahmins: traversing Tartary, it is again found among the Scandinavians, the Germans, and the Celts. Pliny relates that the Druids wore white vestments, and sacrificed oxen of this colour[a].

Finally the Christian painters of the middle ages represent the Eternal draped in white, and likewise Jesus Christ, after the resurrection[b]. The chief of the Roman Church, the Pope, wears on earth the livery of God.

In the sacred language of the Bible, white vestments are the symbols of the regeneration of souls, and the recompense of the elect. He who conquers, says the Apocalypse, shall be clothed in white, and I will not efface his name from the book of life, the kingdom of Heaven belongs to those who have washed and whitened their robes in the blood of the Lamb[c].

White was consecrated to the dead by all antiquity, and became a colour of mourning. The monuments of Thebes represent the shades of the departed clothed in white robes[d]. According to Herodotus, the Egyptians enveloped the dead in white sheets[e]. This custom is found in Greece, from the highest antiquity: Homer mentions it at the death of Patroclus[f]; Pythagoras orders its observance to his disciples, as a happy presage of immortality[g]; Plutarch recalls the doctrine of this philosopher, and explains the symbol which was customary throughout Greece.

Pausanias observed the same custom among the Messenians; they enshrouded chief personages in white vestments and crowned them[h]. This double symbol indicated the triumph of the soul over the empire of darknesses.

The Hebrews had the same custom[i]. The Evangelist Matthew says that Joseph, having taken the body of the Lord, wrapped it in a white linen cloth[k]. The example offered by the divinity became the law of all Christians; the poet Prudentius establishes the practice in one of his hymns, and it is unvaried in our own times.

The initiation or regeneration of the soul commences by an image of death; the mystics were clothed in white, and the neophytes of the primitive church wore a

---

[a] Plinii, lib. xvi. et xxiv.
[b] St. Mark, cap. xvi. 5; St. Luke, xxiv. 4; St. John, xx. 12.
[c] Apocalypsis, cap. iii. 4, 5; vii. 14; xxii. 14.
[d] Description de l'Égypte, planches.
[e] Herod. lib. ii. cap. 81.
[f] Iliad Σ.
[g] Jamblichus de vita Pythag. Num. clv.
[h] Pausanias, in Messen. lib. iv.
[i] Buxtorf Scol. Jud. cap. xlix.
[k] Matth. cap. xxvii. 59.

white robe during eight days[a]. Young girls, catechumens, still wear it, and in the obsequies of virgins white draperies testify their innocence and celestial initiation.

It is useless to pursue the history of these rites in the east; it suffices to cite an example borrowed from the Japanese customs. In Japan marriage is considered as a new existence for the female; she dies to her past life, to revive in her husband. The bed of the betrothed is placed with the pillow towards the north, similar to the practice for the dead; she wears the white mortuary robe. This ceremony announces to the parents that they are about to lose their daughter[b].

PROFANE LANGUAGE.

Religions, led away by their tendency to materialism, formed special divisions of each of the attributes of God; Paganism broke this limit, and the virtues and vices of men found their types in heaven; the Greeks and Romans raised altars to faith and to truth.

Primitive faith addresses itself to God only, and found its emblem in the colour affecting the divine unity, white; profane faith, which presides over human transactions, good faith preserved the symbol of the relations between the Creator and the creature.

Numa consecrated a temple to this deified virtue; she was represented clothed in white, with hands joined; the sacrifices offered to her were without effusion of blood, by priests or flamens covered with white veils, and the hand enveloped in a white cloth. The united hands were the emblem of faith, as may be observed on antique monuments.

The origin of this divinity cannot appear doubtful, in considering the progressive march of religious degradation in the god Fidius, the god of contracts, born from the prostitution of a dancer with a priest of Mars Enialius.

Human truth, deified by the Greeks and Romans, had likewise white vestments[c].

Descending one degree more in the history of the Symbolism of Colours: it is again found in popular languages,—the relics of the divine and the consecrated languages.

The Greek word *leukos* signifies white, happy, agreeable, gay: Jupiter had the surname *Leuceus:* in Latin, *candidus*, white, candid, and happy. The Romans marked auspicious days with chalk, inauspicious days with charcoal[d]. The word

---

[a] Solerius de Pileo.
[b] Tatsingh, Ceremonies in Japan.
[c] Philostrat. in Amphiarao.
[d] Persius; Horace, Sat. v. &c.

candidate has the same origin. He who solicited popular favours at Rome wore a white robe, or one whitened with chalk.

In the German language we find the words *weiss*, white, and *wissen*, to know; *ich weiss*, I know: in English, white, and wit, spirit, witty, spiritual wisdom. The Druids were white men, wise and learned.

These etymologies are confirmed by the popular signification of white colour: the Moors designate by this emblem, purity, sincerity, innocence, indifference, simplicity, candour; applied to a woman, it implies chastity; to a young girl, virginity; to a judge, integrity; to a rich man, humility[a].

Heraldry, borrowing this catalogue, ordained that in coats of arms, argent should denote whiteness, purity, hope, truth, and innocence. Ermine, which was at first all white, was the emblem of purity, and of immaculate chastity[b]; and we hold, says Lamothe Le Vayer[c], the whiteness of our lily, of our scarfs, and royal pennant, a symbol of purity as well as of liberty. White represents immaculate chastity,—it was consecrated to the Virgin; her altars are white, the ornaments of the officiating priest are white, and likewise, on her festival day, the clergy are in white.

Popular traditions and ancient legends offer an ample harvest to our researches: I shall limit myself to explain the hidden sense of some fabulous or symbolic stones.

The Bible presents the type of the language of colours in all its purity. Jesus says in the Apocalypse, I will give to the victorious a white stone, on which shall be written a new name, which no one can know but he who receives it[d]. The white stone is the emblem of truth, united with righteousness and confirmed by works[e]. In confirmative suffrages, the ancients gave white pebbles. The name indicates the quality of the thing,—a new name is a quality of good which as yet does not exist.

The marvellous virtues that antiquity attributed to certain precious stones, is explicable on the same principle.

The diamond, says superstition, calms anger, binds the married in union: it is named the stone of reconciliation[f]. Wisdom, innocence, and faith, indicated by the whiteness and the purity of this stone, appease anger, bind conjugal affection,

---

[a] Gassier, Histoire de la Chevalerie française, pp. 351, 352. The Chinese, likewise, attribute white to justice.—Visdelou, Notice sur l'Y-King à la suite du Chou-King, p. 428.

[b] Anselme, Palais de l'Honneur, pp. 11 and 12. Colombière, Science héroïque, p. 34.

[c] Opuscules, p. 227, 6d. de Paris, 1647.

[d] Apocalypse, ii. 17.

[e] Opaque white indicates the third degree, which is the union of the good and the true in action.—Vide the "Principles."

[f] Noël, Dict. de la Fable.

and reconcile man with God.   In Iconologic language, according to Noël, the diamond is the symbol of constancy, of power, of innocence, and other heroic virtues.

Popular tales recount that diamonds produce diamonds.   Ruens pretends that a princess of Luxemburgh possessed an hereditary family of them.   Do we not recognise in this, that wisdom is transmitted from ancestors, and engenders all the virtues?

Epiphanius wrote that the chief priest of Israel wore a diamond when he entered into the sanctuary, at the three grand festivals of the year.   This stone shone with the brilliancy of snow when announcing an auspicious event: it appeared red as blood at approaching war, and black when general woe was near[a].   Here is found again the altered tradition of the Urim and Thummim, which manifested the divine responsions by the variations of light.

The ancients pretended that there was found in the Red Sea a precious stone white as silver, almost as the diamond: its form was square as a die.   Pliny and Isidorus name it Androdamas: it appeased anger and the emotions of the soul[b].

The cube was, like white colour, the symbol of truth, of wisdom, and of moral perfection.   The New Jerusalem, promised in the Apocalypse, is equal in length, breadth, and height.   This mystical city ought to be considered as a new church, where divine wisdom will reign.   Isaiah, announcing the coming of the Messiah, said, He shall dwell in the highest place of the solid rock, and the water which shall flow from him shall give life.   I have borrowed this quotation from the Catholic epistles of St. Barnabas, who implies that all the words of the Bible are symbolic.

It would be superfluous to reproduce the doctrine of Pythagoras on numbers, a doctrine evidently borrowed from the Egyptians, and which coincides, partly at least, with the symbolism of the Bible.   The number 4, according to this philosopher, is the divinity, the source of nature: four possesses in itself all the numbers, as the cube contains all the forms[c].

The book of Esther mentions a stone named *dar*.   The Rabbis pretend that it is found in the sea, and that, presented in a festival, it displays the light of the noonday sun.   To obtain it, kings grant freedom to the possessor, and give him immense riches[d].   This stone is a new symbol of wisdom: it is found, like the Androdamas,

---

[a] St. Epiphanius de xii. gemmis.

[b] Isid. Orig. lib. xvi. cap. 14.

[c] Origenis philosophumena, p. 34. Hierocles Aurea Carmina, p. 219. Compare on this doctrine Eckartshaüsens Aufschlüsse sur Magie, and St. Martin, of Truth and Error.

[d] Caussin, Symbolica, p. 621.

in the depths of the sea; and the sea was, amongst every nation, as we shall establish, the symbol of entry into the church; of initiation by baptism.

The ararophylax, according to Plutarch[a], is a precious stone like unto silver; those who are rich buy it and place it at the entrance of their treasuries. When thieves come, this stone makes the sound of a trumpet, and the malefactors, overpowered by an irresistible force, are precipitated afar. Silver is by its brightness the symbol of divine wisdom, as gold is of divine love. The Apocalypse here explains Plutarch. I counsel you, says St. John, to buy gold proved in the fire to enrich you, and white vestments to clothe you, i. e. to acquire the love of God and wisdom. The sound of the trumpet which is heard from this stone, recalls that which sounds in the festivals of the Jewish people; and the trumpets of the last judgment. The Lord Jehovah, says Zechariah[b], shall sound the trumpet, i. e. will manifest, his wisdom; any one must be insensible to read these passages literally.

Pliny relates that the stone named chernites is like ivory; it preserves the body from any corruption: the tomb of Darius was of chernites because of this virtue[c]. Among the Egyptians the manes were clothed in white; as the phantoms of our popular tales. The Apocalypse promises white robes to those who overcome, and will be no more subjected to the second death; and white winding sheets, like white sepulchres, as well as mourning worn white, testify the doctrine of the immortality of the soul. Ivory was the symbol of truth because of its shining whiteness. True dreams issue from the shades by the ivory gate, and false visions by the gate of horn.

The leucas or white stone cures love[d], as wisdom curbs the passions. The stone myndan is surrounded with the whiteness of snow; it drives away ferocious beasts and secures man from their bite[e], as innocence and wisdom dissipate evil thoughts and prevent their dreadful consequences.

The poem of Orpheus on stones, or the *Peri-lithon*, remains to this day an undecipherable enigma; this precious monument of antiquity is written entirely in symbolic language, and apparently anterior to the hymns and 'Argonautics attributed to the same poet. Orpheus firstly describes the marvellous properties of two white stones, the diamond and the crystal, which generate every good and every virtue, as white

[a] Plutarch de fluminibus.
[b] Zechariah ix. 14.
[c] Plinii lib. 36, cap. 16.   Theophrasti Eresii de lapidibus, p. 2.
[d] Caussin Symbolica, p. 629.
[e] Leont. Byzant. lib. iii. de Fluviis.

holds in itself the principle of all colours ; crystal is the source of flame [a], as wisdom gives birth to divine love. By this example, one perceives the impossibility of understanding a single passage of the *Peri-lithon* before acquiring the symbolism of colours and of stones which correspond to them.

The catalogue of colours is very restricted, but however, they may express a great number of ideas, in receiving different acceptations according to the objects to which they are applied. White, the symbol of the divinity and of priesthood, represents divine wisdom; applied to a young girl it denotes virginity; to an accused person, innocence; to a judge, justice; as a characteristic sign of purity it exhibits a promise of hope after death;—opposed to black, the emblem of darkness, of grief, of anguish; white is the colour for festivals in which Roman convivialists appeared.

OF YELLOW.

DIVINE LANGUAGE.

" In the beginning," said St. John, " was the Word, and the Word was with God, and the Word was God. He was in the beginning with God. All things were made by Him and without Him was not any thing made that was made. In Him was life, and the life was the light of men, and the light shines in the darkness, and the darkness comprehended it not." [b]

This celestial light revealed to men, finds its natural symbol in the light which shines on earth; the heat and the brightness of the sun designate the love of God which animates the heart, and the wisdom which enlightens the intellect. These two attributes of God manifest in the creation of the world and the regeneration of men, appear inseparable in the signification of the sun, of gold, and yellow. Divine wisdom had white for a symbol, as divine love, red; golden yellow reunites these two significations and forms them into one; but with the character of manifestation and revelation. This explains an ancient tradition current in emblazonry: authors on the heraldic art pretend that the yellow colour is a mixture of red and white [c].

In the Bible, the sun represents love divine, when it is opposed to the moon, symbol of wisdom; it is likewise of the gold which indicates the goodness of God, opposed to silver, emblem of divine truth.

The sun, the gold, and the yellow, are not synonymes, but mark different degrees, which it is difficult to determine precisely. The natural sun was the symbol of

---

[a] Αὐτὸς ὅτις τέλεται φλογὸς αἴτιος.—Orphei Crystallus.

[b] St. John, ch. i.

[c] La Colombière, Science héroïque, p. 28, 29.

the spiritual sun. Gold expressed the natural sun, and yellow was the emblem of gold [a].

All religions rest on these symbols as bases of their dogmas.

In the beginning, said the Persians, the Word was created by the union of primitive fire and primitive water. Ormus decreed it and the chief of darkness was overcome; from the Holy Word primitive light emanated, which, in its turn, created visible light, water and fire. Honover is the Word; in his essence he is confounded with Ormus the god creator; in the second degree he appeared under the form of the tree of life, Hom; finally, in his third degree he is the annunciator of the Word, and under the same name of Hom, or Homanes, founds magiism under the great Dschemschid [b].

Mithras is the sacerdotal personification of this dogma. The esoteric doctrine sees in him the unity anterior to the dualism of Ormus and Ahriman; he was the eternal himself, Zervane Akerene, whilst the popular creed tends to identify him with the sun his symbol.

Mithras is the divine idea, the Word or the speech of God revealed to the inhabitants of Persia, the source of all light; gold and yellow colour are his attributes, like those of Apollo.

The first of celestial genii, Mithras, is mounted on the redoubtable Albordy, an immortal vigorous courser, he dwells at a mountain of gold; with his golden mace he strikes impure spirits; victorious he is seated on a cloth of gold, he himself is of the colour of gold.

Again Mithras is the mediator, the executor of the holy word; he watches over the dead; it is by his celestial influence that man elevates himself in his thoughts, words and actions, and imagines no evil. He succours him who abandons evil ways, and invokes him with pure hands; he weighs the actions of men on the bridge of eternity, which separates heaven from earth [c].

The first Christians, afraid of the perfect identity of symbols and of the ceremonies of Christianity and of Mithraism, attributed its cause to the Spirit of Darknesses; they did not accuse the followers of Mithras of having borrowed their mysteries

[a] Heraldry again presents a proof. La Colombière, in remarking the relation which exists between gold and yellow, and between silver and white, says, that as the yellow from the sun may be called the highest of colours, so gold is the noblest of metals; thus, says he further, sages have called it the son of the sun. Silver is as respects gold what the moon is to the sun, and as these two planets hold the first rank amongst others, so gold and silver excel the rest of the metals.

[b] Creuzer, Religions de l'Antiquité, tome i. pp. 321 et 343. Vendidad Sadé, pp. 138, 140. Here reappear the three degrees discussed in the chapter on principles.

[c] Zent-Avesta, iescht de Mithra et passim.

from the worship of the Messiah, they knew that the Persian doctrine was anterior; the devil cut the Gordian knot[a], as in our days Dupuis solved the difficulty by the worship of the sun. The promise of a redeemer prevailed throughout the East, and the symbolic genius which personified prophecies as well as doctrines, alone offered the solution of this problem.

Zoroaster was not the inventor of the religion which bears his name, but the reformer of the ancient worship consecrated to the spiritual Sun; his name signifies, star of gold, brilliant, liberal, shining star[b]; the qualification of Zeré or golden given likewise to Hom, the divine word, conducts us into India, where we find the same dogmas[c].

According to the Bagavadam Vischnou is the first emanation of God, He is the Spiritual Sun, the eternal thought, the word divine, God shining in light, He moved on the surface of the water; whence He acquired the name of Narayana[d], one of his epithets is wearer of yellow robes[e]. Vischnou is incarnate in Krichna, the revealed word.

The laws of Manou attribute to Brahma the character which Vischnou performs in the Bagavadam, that which the spirit only can perceive; having resolved in his mind, to cause the various creatures to emanate from his substance, produced at first the waters, in which he deposited a seed; this germ became an egg brilliant as gold, thus shining as a star with a thousand rays, and in which the Supreme Being created himself under the form of Brahma, the grandsire of all other existences; Brahma is likewise named Narayana, he who moved over the waters[f].

Vischnou the Supreme Being, and Brahma his first manifestation, often appear confounded as God and the Eternal Word.

Egypt reproduces the same dogma. The Pimander, of which the mysterious

[a] Sed quæritur a quo intellectus intervertatur eorum quæ ad hæreses faciunt? A diabolo scilicet . . . . . Tingit et ipse quosdam utique credentes et fideles suos, expositionem delictorum de lavacro repromittit, et sic adhuc initiat Milthræ. Signat illis in frontibus milites suos; celebrat et panis oblationem, et imaginem resurrectionis inducit, et sub gladio redimit coronam. Tertulliani de præscriptionibus, cap. 40.

[b] Zéréthoschtrô, de Zéré qui signifie doré ou d'or. (Anquetil, sur le Zent-Avesta, t. i. part 2. p. 4.) Zerdusht, dancing forth into joy at the appearance of the light. D. Morison's Religious History of Man.

[c] Om, the Indian Trinity. Hom is of the colour of gold; those who eat it annihilate evil. Vendidad Sadé, p. 114.

[d] Bagavadam, pp. 46, 48, 62.

[e] Paulin, Systema Bramanicum, p. 80.

[f] Lois de Manou, liv. i. and Sir William Jones, on the Gods of India, iii. 353. The same cosmogony was adopted by the Tartars, if they were not the first possessors of it. In the beginning, say they, there existed an enormous space, clouds of the colour of gold collected together, and there was so great an abundance of rain that there was formed an immense sea. (Histoire des découvertes dans plusieurs Contrées de la Russie, vi. 133.)

name indicates the word revealed to the Egyptians by Amon, or the Word, contains textually the doctrine of St. John. The light, says he, is myself, God—Intellect,—more ancient than the humid principle, which shone in darkness; and the word irradiating from the Intellect is the Son of God, and the Intellect itself is God the Father; they are never separate, for their union is the life [a]. It has been pretended that this doctrine was the work of neoplatonism. How then is it again found consecrated by the Egyptian Mythology?

Amon was the light revealed, the Word divine. Iamblichus says that in the mysteries of Egypt, the Supreme Being, the God of truth and of wisdom, took the name of Amon when he revealed himself to the world in his divine light [b].

The revelation personified and separated from the Divinity by the Intellect became the Son of God; Horus, son of Osiris and of Isis, is born from the union of mind and matter, as the word of the religion of the Persians Honover.

The name of Horus or Hor, is again found in that portion of Genesis where God says light shall be, and light was, (אור, Aur, light. Genesis ch. i. and 3rd verse.) Horus, the Word divine, presides at the creation of the world; he was born like Brahma, in the bosom of the waters, and in the calyx of a lotus [c]. The birth of the sun was represented in like manner.

Gold was consecrated to Horus as to Vischnou and to Mithras; the resemblance between the Latin word *aurum*, the French *or*, and the Hebrew *aor*, light, indicates it, and monuments demonstrate it.

Vischnou, Mithras, Horus, and Apollo, are the same divinity, representative of one and the same dogma. This myth issuing from the east, materializes itself in its course towards the west and the south; in India, Vischnou is completely distinct from the material Sun or Surya, and identifies himself with the mystic sun *Om*. In Zoroastriism, Mithras again approaches to a material worship, at least in his exterior form; in Egypt the symbols of Horus are the same as those appropriated to the sun; finally in Greece, Apollo is the personification of this planet.

The symbol becomes God, the people adore the sun and the heavenly host, Sabeism reigns in the east, then Abraham goes forth from Chaldea, the idols are destroyed, but notwithstanding, the symbols remain the same. Moses appeared to the Israelites shining with light, rays illumined his face; the prophet Habakkuk announces the coming of the Holy One: His splendour, says he, shall shine as a living light, rays shall issue from his hand; it is there where his strength is hidden. The hand was the emblem of power, and the rays of the sun designate the manifestation of

---

[a] Pimander, Sect. v. vi. [b] Iamblich. de mysteriis, p. 159.

[c] Jablonski, Pantheon Ægypt. 212—260.

the love and the wisdom of God. It is not surprising therefore that the Fathers of the Church, by the example of the Prophets, named Jesus Christ, the Light, the Sun, the East [a], and that gold should be his symbol; it is understood why Christian artists gave to Jesus Christ flaxen hair, golden like Apollo's [b], and placed the glory (aureole) on his head, as on that of the Virgin and the Apostles. In Egypt, the circle of gold figured the course of the sun and the accomplishment of the year. The Messiah, the Divine Sun, accomplished a religious and social period, he opened a new era; the crown of glory (aureole) was the natural symbol of an event which perhaps it is reserved to our epoch to appreciate in all its grandeur.

CONSECRATED LANGUAGE.

Gold and yellow received in the consecrated language the particular acceptation of revelation made by the priest, or of religious doctrine taught in the temples. This metal and this colour represented initiation to the mysteries, or the light revealed to the profane.

Anubis is the personification of the Egyptian Initiator; the dog was consecrated to him, because that this god was the guardian of the holy doctrine shut up in the sanctuaries. Egyptian monuments represent him with the head of a dog, and Virgil and Ovid give him the name of a barker, *latrator*. Sirius, or the dog-star, was, according to the Persians, the sentinel of heaven, and the guardian of the gods; the sick implored his aid before dying, and gave from his hand a little food to a dog that was led to his bed; the dog, it was said, was the symbol of the great initiation to the mysteries of death [c].

Colour is the thread of Ariadne, which guides us in the labyrinth of ancient religions; the dog initiator, who strikes and repulses the spirits of darkness, had, according to the Zent-Avesta, the eyes and eyebrows yellow, and ears white and yellow [d].

[a] Splendor autem appellatur propter quod manifestat, lumen quia illuminat, lux quia ad veritatem contemplandam cordis oculos reserat; sol quia illuminat omnes, oriens quia luminis fons et illustrator est rerum et quod oriri nos faciat ad vitam æternam. (Isidori Orig. lib. vii. cap. 2.)

[b] Eustatius pretends that gold was consecrated to Apollo, and that is the reason wherefore Homer gives to this god a sceptre of gold. Millien observes, that Homer says nothing of the appropriation of metals amongst the gods. (Minéralogie Homérique, p. 175.) The testimony of the Scholiast nevertheless remains. Vide, for the attributes of golden or flaxen hair, Junii de pictura veterum, p. 243. "The tunic of Apollo is of gold, his clasp, his lyre, his bow, his quiver, and his buskins are of gold. Gold and riches shine around him; the Pythian attests it." (Callimachus, Hymn to Apollo.)

[c] Creuzer, Religions de l'Antiquité, I. p. 358. Vide statues of the dog at portals of Etruscan tombs.

[d] Zent-Avesta, Vendidad Sadé, pp. 332, 333.

The yellow eye was the emblem of understanding enlightened by revelation, the ears white and yellow figured the instruction of the holy doctrine, which is divine wisdom revealed.

The statues of Anubis were of gold or gilt; the name of this divinity, which is again found in the Coptic language, signifies equally gold or gilt, *Annub*[a].

Anubis, as a personification of the human sciences, took the name of Thot, of which the Greeks make Hermes, and the Romans Mercury.

Mercury Hermanubis is the interpreter and messenger of the gods; he conducts the ghosts into hell; a chain of gold issues from his mouth, and is attached to the ears of those whom he wishes to lead; he holds in his hand a golden rod; one half of his countenance is represented bright and the other half dark, emblems of initiation and of death, where the struggle of the two antagonist principles, light and darkness are reproduced.

Greek art, enamoured by beauty of form, took from Hermanubis his characteristic symbol, the head of the dog; but this animal, separated from the divinity, does not less preserve its sacred signification. The Temple of Vulcan on Etna, it is said, was guarded by dogs. They attracted virtuous men by their caresses, and destroyed the impious[b].

Mercury was the tutelar divinity of thieves; the ancients saw in this attribute a symbol of the mysteries withdrawn from the cognizance of the vulgar[c]; the priests concealed the gold, symbol of the light, from the gaze of the profane.

The fable of the Hesperides offers a novel proof of the signification which is given to gold in the mysteries.

" The Hesperides, according to Hesiod, were daughters of Night, and according to Cherecrates, of Phorcus and of Ceto, divinities of the sea. Juno intermarrying with Jupiter gave him some apple trees which bore golden fruits; these trees were placed in the garden of Hesperides, under the guardianship of a dragon, son of the Earth, according to Pisander; of Typhon and Echidne, according to Pherecydes. This horrible dragon had a hundred heads. The apple trees which he watched incessantly had surprising virtue. It was one of these apples that embroiled the three goddesses

[a] Jablonski, Anubis, p. 19.

[b] This purity of style is lost under the influence of gnosticism, a sect which believes itself to be in possession of the mysteries of antiquity, and which reestablishes a part of its symbols; Mercury reappeared with the head of the dog on the Abraxas. (Macarii Abraxas, Tabula XIII. et passim. Matter, Histoire du Gnosticism, planches.)

[c] . Illi arcanorum scientiam tribuere cupientes, furem tradiderunt esse et vafri Mercurii erexerunt statuam. (Phurnuti de Natura Deorum, p. 157. B.)

in discord. It was with the same fruit that Hippomenes softened the fierce Atalanta. Eurystheus commanded Hercules to seek these apples; Hercules besought the nymphs who dwelt near Eridan to inform him where were the Hesperides; these nymphs sent him back to Nereus, Nereus to Prometheus, who told him what to do. Hercules transported himself into Mauritania, killed the dragon, brought the golden apples to Eurystheus, and thus accomplished the twelfth of his labours."[a]

The golden apples are the fruits of intelligence which are born by the love of God; Juno offers them to Jupiter in uniting herself to him; they are kept in the garden of the Hesperides, daughters of the marine deities, that is to say, in the sanctuary of temples, and confided to the initiated, children of the waters or of baptism. The dragon, the son of Darkness, of Typhon or the Earth, is the emblem of human passions and vices, which permit not the profane to taste of these spiritual fruits. Hercules, or the neophyte, performs the last of his works to seize them. He is sent back to the nymphs, to the marine deities, and at length to Prometheus, who initiates him in the mysteries. Prometheus had formed man from the clay of the earth, and animated him with fire snatched from the celestial bodies. Nereus and Prometheus, or fire and water, recall the double baptism of the antique initiations like those of Christianity.

The sun, gold, and yellow, were the symbols of the human understanding enlightened or illuminated by divine revelation. It is in this sense that the prophet Daniel says, that those who are wise shall be shining with light, and that those who shall influence others to do justly shall shine eternally as the stars[b]. Solomon expresses the same thought in saying that the head of the wise is of the purest gold[c]. Jesus Christ announces that the just shall shine as the sun in the kingdom of his Father[d].

Gold and yellow were in Christian symbolism the emblems of faith[e]. St. Peter, the stay of the church and guardian of the holy doctrine, was represented by the illuminators and miniaturists of the middle ages with a golden yellow robe, and the rod or the key in his hand. These attributes were those of Mercury Hermanubis. In China, yellow is equally the symbol of faith[f].

The ancients compared to gold, that which they judged faultless and exceeding

---

[a] Noël, Dictionnaire de la Fable.
[b] Daniel, cap. xii. 3.
[c] Caput ejus aurum optimum: (Cantic. cap. v. 11.)
[d] St. Matth. xiii. 43.
[e] La Colombière, Science héroïque, p. 35.
[f] Visdelou, Notice sur l'Y-King à la Suite du Chou-King, p. 436.

beautiful; by the age of gold they understood the age of happiness and virtue, and by the golden verses, according to Hierocles, verses in which the purest doctrine was contained[a]. We again meet with this tradition in the golden legends of the saints.

Food of a golden yellow colour became emblematic of the love and of the wisdom of God which man appropriates to himself, or *eats*, to speak symbolically. The divine poet Isaiah says, that he who shall refuse the evil and choose the good shall eat of butter and of honey[b]. Job exclaims that the wicked shall not see the floods of butter and of honey[c]. In the song of songs, Solomon addresses his mystic spouse, whose lips distil as a honeycomb[d]: thus, in the Iliad, from the mouth of the sage Nestor, words dropped sweeter than honey[e]. Pindar borrowed the same image when he said that conquerors shall dwell in a land abounding in honey.

Virgil calls honey the celestial gift distilled from the dew[f], and dew was the emblem of initiation[g]. Pliny gives it the epithet, the effusion from heaven, the saliva of the stars[h].

The symbol of divine revelation became that of sacred and poetic inspiration; the Melissa or Bees were inspired women who prophesied in the temples of Greece; popular legends narrate that bees reposed on the lips of Plato in his cradle; and that Pindar, when exposed in the woods in his infancy, was nourished with honey: the first Christians and the disciples of Mithras gave honey to be tasted by the mystics, and made them wash their hands with honey[i]. Cakes of honey were offered in sacrifice by most nations of antiquity.

The sweetness of this aliment was doubtless one of the motives of its symbolic attribution, but the colour of it was the principal basis. Ovid wishing to express that wisdom enlightens the understanding, gives to Minerva the epithet of yellow—flava Minerva[k]. On the contrary, unwholesome and wild aliments took by their golden colour an inverse signification. The precursor of the Messiah came to

---

[a] Hierocles, Comment. in aur. carmin. præm.

[b] Butyrum et mel comedet, ut sciet reprobare malum et eligere bonum. (Isai. cap. vii. 15.)

[c] Job. cap. xx. 17.

[d] Cant. iv. 11.

[e] Iliados A. 249.

[f] Georg. iv. 1.

[g] Vide of Rose colour.

[h] Plin. lib. xi. cap. 12. Comp. Theophrasti Eresii Opera, p. 296.

[i] Explication de divers monumens singuliers.

[k] Ovidii Metamorph. et Amor. This tint was that of honey water, mella flava, says Martial, (lib. i. 56,) or golden yellow.

announce a new revelation at the epoch when the ancient was forgotten or misunderstood, and in the desert he was fed with locusts and wild honey. This exhibits the first example of the rule of oppositions.

In a celestial sense, light, gold, and yellow, evince divine love enlightening the human understanding; in the infernal sense it denotes that odiously proud egotism which seeks not wisdom but in itself, which becomes its own god, its own principle, and end.

According to St. Paul, Satan transforms himself into an angel of light [a]. Jesus Christ says, Beware that the light which is in you be not darkness [b]. In this state of separation from God and isolation, man commits adultery, he sullies his soul by an earthly love, which he ought to offer up pure to his Creator. In the symbolism of the Bible, Sodom is the figure of that degradation which at its last boundaries betrays him into infamous crimes. Sulphur represents the same idea, because of its colour and combustion, which generates a suffocating smoke [c].

The rain of sulphur which consumed Sodom, is the strong image of depraved passions which devour the heart of the impious and brutalize their intellect. In the day that Lot went out of Sodom, says Jesus Christ, a rain of fire and of sulphur fell from heaven and destroyed all; it will be the same in that day when the Son of Man shall appear, whosoever will seek to save his life shall lose it, and whosoever will lose it shall save it [d]. Thus, when human passions shall have degraded religious belief, the divinity will manifest himself anew on the earth, those who will attach themselves to terrestrial life, shall lose life eternal—the life of the soul; and those who renounce worldly existence shall save their spiritual existence.

The sense which I assign to the word sulphur is absolute, and in the Bible is without any exception; the light of the wicked, says Job, shall be put out, and their fire shall not glimmer; the light which lightens their houses shall be obscure, and their lamp shall be extinct; God will shower *sulphur* upon the place where they make their dwelling—they shall be chased from the light into darkness—they will be banished from the world [e]. The Psalmist, the Prophets, and the Apocalypse confirm the signification of this symbol.

Lastly, in Paganism sulphur was employed for purification of the guilty, because it was the symbol of guilt [f].

---

[a] 2 Corinth. xi. 14.
[b] Luke, xi. 35.
[c] On the symbol of Smoke, vide Tan Colour.
[d] Luke, xvii.
[e] Job, xviii.
[f] Noël, Dict. de la Fable, verb. Soufre.

PROFANE LANGUAGE.

The divine and consecrated languages designate by gold and yellow the union of the soul to God; and by opposition, spiritual adultery. In the profane language, this materialized emblem represents legitimate love and carnal adultery, which breaks the marriage ties.

Jesus Christ says that divorce is not permitted but in case of adultery, and we find, in this human law the image of the divine law, which wills that man shall not be separated from his Creator but by egotism, as he is eternally united to him by love and charity.

The golden apple was, among the Greeks, the emblem of love and concord, and by opposition, it designated discord and all the evils which follow in its train[a]; the judgment of Paris is a proof of it Likewise Atalanta in again risking the apples of gold gathered in the gardens of the Hesperides is conquered in the course and becomes the prize of the victory.

The symbolism of the middle ages preserved with purity the traditions of the yellow colour; the Moors distinguish in them two symbols, opposed by two different gradations of colour; the golden yellow signifies *the wise and of good counsel*, and the pale yellow *treason and deception*[b]. The Rabbis pretend that the fruit of the forbidden tree was a citron[c], by an opposition of its pale colour and of its acidity with the golden colour and the sweetness of the orange or golden apple, according to the Latin expression.

In blazonry, gold is the emblem of love, of constancy, and of wisdom[d]; and by opposition, yellow still, in our days, denotes inconstancy, jealousy, and adultery.

[a] Creuzer, Aphrodite, p. 660.

[b] Gassier, de la Chevalerie.

[c] Ferarii Hesperides, sive de malorum aureorum, p. 39.

[d] Anselme, Palais de l'Honneur, p. 11. Bonif. Historia ludicra, Lib. I. cap. xi. La Colombière, in his Traité du Blason, says, that gold corresponds with the sun, and with the heart, and that the same relation exists between silver, the moon, and the brain. This passage is curious, because it offers the symbolic signification of white and of yellow, during the middle ages. Yellow, or gold, corresponding to the heart, designates love; white, or silver, emblem of the brain, signifies wisdom: the sun and the moon, gold and silver, the heart and the brain, preserve herein the symbolic attributes transmitted by antiquity. — Science héroïques, p. 31.

Gold, in coats of arms, says the same author, indicates of the Christian virtues, faith; of mundane qualities, love and constancy; of precious stones, the carbuncle; of the four elements, fire; of the complexions of men, the sanguine; of the days of the week, Sunday. [Ibid. p. 34.] The carbuncle and fire were in symbolic correspondence with yellow, because that this colour, according to La Colombière, is composed from red and white. The golden ring, given in marriage, and on obtaining offices of trust and confidence, confirms this.

In several countries, the law ordains that Jews be clothed in yellow, because they had betrayed the Lord : in France, the door of traitors was daubed with yellow. Under Francis I., Charles de Bourbon incurred this disgrace for the crime of felony[a].

On the windows of the church of Ceffonds in Champagne, which date from the 16th century, Judas is clothed in yellow; in Spain, the vestments of the executioner ought to be red or yellow : the yellow indicates the treason of the guilty, and the red his punishment.

It becomes easy, by understanding these chief colours, to comprehend the signification of the four ages, represented by the four metals ; the Golden Age, the Silver Age, the Brazen Age, and the Iron Age.

Gold is the symbol of divine love revealed to man; silver, by its white colour, designates divine wisdom; brass or copper, false gold, denotes degraded love, or religion materialized[b]; iron, by its sombre grey colour, indicates wisdom perverted and truth misunderstood[c].

It is thus the statue described in the book of Daniel is explained ; his head was of refined gold, his breast and his arms of silver, his belly and his thighs of brass, and his feet of clay and of iron[d].

In applying this ancient tradition to the history of humanity, there appears, up to Christianity, four religious periods corresponding to the signification of four metals : this investigation would require a special work ; but it is easy to establish the existence of the universal law in the history of every religion.

A new divine revelation is at first marked by the love which creates martyrs ; at this period the holy succeeds the divine wisdom,—the consecrated epoch, in which are born the Hermes in Egypt, the Prophets in Israel, the Fathers of the Church in

---

[a] La Mothe-le-Vayer, Opuscules, p. 240.

[b] Brass, in the Bible, represents the last degree, or the natural ; applied to man, it indicates the body ; applied to religion, it denotes the letter which is the body of the spirit. The adoration of the letter is the last term of all religions ; thus Symbolism created Paganism. Judaism perished in the same manner. The letter kills, says the Evangelist, and the spirit vivifies. So John, in the Apocalypse, saw Jesus Christ with feet like fine brass, when in a burning furnace.—Apoc. i. 15. Martianus Capella says, that the God Sun, that is to say, the mystic sun, was shod with fine brass. (Compare the learned and beautiful work of Richer, de la Nouvelle Jerusalem, t. ii. p. 149.) In Paganism, religious instruments were generally of brass, as Millin remarks in his Minéralogie Homérique, p. 141. Servius says, that this metal is more agreeable to the gods. (In Æneid. 1.) The instruments of Mosaic worship were all of brass, (Basnage, ii. 245.) because it represented religion in its last degree in material worship. Likewise the brazen sea, the brazen altar for holocausts, signified the natural of man, which ought to be purified by water, and regenerated by the sacrifice of passions, represented by the victims offered.

[c] The threshold of hell is of brass, said Homer, and the gates are of iron.—(Iliad. viii. 15.)

[d] Daniel, ii. 31.

Christianity; the profane æra, the age of brass, materializes worship; idolatry arises, extends its roots, and stifles religious truth; the iron age, the age of dissolution, appears, the age of human wisdom, which seeks not light but in itself, turns into derision the altered faith, examines creeds only in their degradation, and saps the feet of iron and of clay of the Colossus, which falls and is shattered.

The history of religions, and of schools of philosophy, does not enter into the plan of this work; but I must cast one glance on Paganism, to find again, in the Sophists of the 18th century, the degrading philosophy of the last days of Greece and Rome.

To the epoch of dissolution and annihilation, succeeds a new religious æra,— a new golden age: the society, which is extinct, announced it to future generations, the prophetic voice of Rome retained in the immortal verses of Virgil, and in our own days, the universal expectation vibrates in the stanzas of a modern poet :—

> Réveille nous, grand Dieu! parle, et change le monde;
> Fais entendre au néant ta parole féconde,
> Il est temps! lève toi! Sors de ce long repos;
> Tire un autre univers de cet autre chaos.—*Lamartine, Méditations Religieuses.*

 END OF FIRST SECTION.

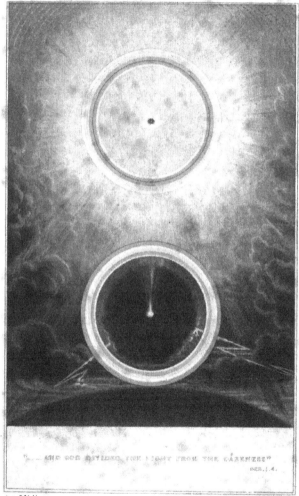

"... AND GOD DIVIDED THE LIGHT FROM THE DARKNESS."

GEN. I. 4.

SYMBOLIC COLOURS,

IN ANTIQUITY—THE MIDDLE AGES—AND MODERN TIMES.

FROM THE FRENCH OF FRÉDÉRIC PORTAL.

WITH NOTES.

BY W. S. INMAN, Assoc.Inst. Civil Engineers.

SECOND SECTION.

OF RED.

DIVINE LANGUAGE.

WHITE is the symbol of God, gold and yellow indicate the Word, or Revelation, and red and blue, the Holy Ghost, or Sanctification. In his unity God created the universe, as the Son of God he revealed himself to men, as the Holy Ghost he regenerates them by love and truth; it is in this sense that St. Cyril names him the fruit of the divine essence[a]. The Holy Ghost is God manifesting himself in the heart and enlightening the faithful; he is the love proceeding from the Creator, the baptism of fire and of the spirit; of love and of truth.

From these principles a singular interpretation of the sacred books of ancient nations is deduced. In pagan cosmogonies, as in Genesis, the world is created by the Spirit of God and the Holy Spirit, or Holy Ghost; but the Holy Ghost being the sanctification of man by God, it is evident that these cosmogonies are the symbol of the formation of the universe, treating of the regeneration of man. The confirmation of this fact is seen in the initiation to the mysteries, whose aim was the spiritual birth of the Neophyte, and whose rites typified the creation of the world.

[a] Cyrilli Thesauri, lib. xiii. cap. 3.

A fresh proof results from this frequent comparison of the world and of man, of macrocosm and microcosm, its image.

The doctrine here exhibited has been supported by Picus Mirandula [a], and confirmed by Swedenborg, in the celestial Arcana. The mythological names of the week, and the assigning of colours to the planets, are additional proofs, which will be developed in the explanation of monuments.

The Holy Ghost is God manifesting himself in his church and in regenerated man. The gospel is herein confirmed by the sacred traditions of the most ancient nations.

If it be true, as modern discoveries in archæology indicate, that mankind have descended from the table-land of Upper Asia, the religion of Bouddha may, perhaps, still preserve some tenets of primitive worship. The numerous points of resemblance which exist between Christianity and Bouddhism, are evidence of our system. Bouddha is not the name of a man but God, revealing himself to the world by the intermediation of holy personages, who have identified and assimilated themselves to his essence, and have taken his name. Shakia-Mouni, named Bouddha in India, and Fo in China, is not the founder of this worship, but the seventh reformer, or Bouddhist prophet [b].

The tri-unity, or divine trinity, is the fundamental tenet of Bouddhism. The name of this triad is Om! as in Brahmanism.

Bouddha is the Supreme Being, d'Harma the law, and Sanga the union; these three beings make but one.

In the interior doctrine Bouddha has produced the law, both reunited have constituted the union,—the bond of several. In the public doctrine these three terms are still Bouddha, or the intellect; the law and the union; but considered in their exterior manifestation, the intellect in the expected Bouddha; the law in the revealed scripture; and the union, or the multiplicity in the reunion of the faithful, or the assembly of priests (ecclesia).

M. Abel Remusat reunites this doctrine in these two tables:

INTERIOR, OR THEOLOGIC DOCTRINE.

The Intellect.—The Logos, or the Word.—The Union.

EXTERIOR DOCTRINE, OR WORSHIP.

Bouddha.—Revelation.—The Church.

---

[a] Pici Mirandulæ, Heptaplus de opere sex dierum Geneseos.
[b] Abel Remusat, de la Triade suprème chez les Bouddhistes, pp. 25, 26.

The philosopher from whom I select these curious documents, adds, that the Chinese consider Fo, the law and the union, as cosubstantial, and of one nature in three substances.

Sanga, or the Holy Spirit, proceeds from God and the Word; and this tenet again appears in Christianity. Sanga is the union of man to God, and the Holy Ghost in the Gospel, is the love and truth of God animating the heart and enlightening the spirit of the apostles. In the most intimate sense, the Word is the Creator, and the Holy Ghost the regenerator. All beings emanate from the bosom of the Divinity by the Word; but man only, animated by the Holy Spirit, refers to his Creator the love which has given him life.

The sacred books of India reproduce this primitive and Christian doctrine. When by means of celestial fire, of the fire supreme, says the Yadjour-Veda, heaven is entered, the inhabitants of these high places taste the fruit of immortality. The celestial fire is the incorporated spirit which rests in the cavity at the centre of the heart. It is the foundation of the universe; it is that by which the boundless world is attained; it is the principle and the origin of worlds. The fire of sacrifices is the symbol of this celestial fire[a]. It is impossible here to misunderstand the Sanga of the Bouddhists and the Holy Ghost of Christians,—creator of the universe and regenerator of man by love and truth. Fire and ether are symbols of the incorporated spirit[b]. Thus the colours red and azure are assigned to the cosmogonic divinities, Vischnou and Brahma.

This doctrine of a surpassing purity, is translated in Genesis by identical symbols. Jehovah God formed man of the dust of the ground, and *breathed* into his nostrils the breath of life; and he made man a living soul. The spirit of life is love divine and truth divine, or faith; man was therefore created by the Holy Ghost, or by love and truth. Humanity is the receptacle of divine love, and his Hebrew name signifies red, Adam[c].

In the Bible, the wind, air, ether, and its colour, blue, are symbols of the spirit of truth; fire, and its colour, red, represent divine love. The Spirit of God moved over chaos. By the word of the LORD were the heavens made, said the prophet king,

[a] Nathaka-Oupanichat, extrait du Yadjour-Veda, traduit par Poley.

[b] Colebrooke's Philosophy of the Hindoos, pp. 170, 171. Brahma, the creator of the world, was born in the calyx of a lotus, and this lotus is in the heart. He appears as fire and as ether, symbol of the Holy Spirit, in his double attribute of love and of wisdom.

[c] אדם Adam, the man of אדם, he reddened (or was ruddy), or rather of אדם, which the Seventy translate by πυῤῥὸς, colour of fire, "Adam, Sicut beatus Hieronymus tradidit, homo sive terrenus: sive terra rubra interpretatur." (Isidori Originum, liber vii. cap. 6.)

and all the host of them by the breath, or inspiration of his mouth [a]. The anointed of the Lord is called the breath of his nostrils; because he is eternal truth. He breathed on his disciples and said to them, Receive the Holy Ghost [b], that is to say, the truth by love. When the Holy Ghost descended on the apostles, there was suddenly heard a great sound, as of a rushing mighty wind, which came from heaven, and it filled all the house where they were sitting: and there appeared unto them cloven tongues like as of fire, and it sat upon each of them [c].

In all sacred writings a relationship is recognised; all are animated with the same spiritual thoughts, although veiled in different symbolic forms. The Pimander will enable us to understand the secret doctrine of these ancient codes, and perhaps give the interpretation of some hieroglyphs.

Hermes, wrapped in ecstacy, saw Amon, or the Divine Word appear, and say, I am Pimander, the mind of him who is self-existing, I know thy thoughts, and am everywhere with thee. I desire, answered Hermes, to learn that which is; to comprehend the nature of things, and to know God. Then the mystery of the creation of the world moves the spirit of the Egyptian prophet; he declares, " All things became light, and in my wonder I was embraced by love; darknesses, " terrible and odious, were suppressed, and it seemed to me that they changed " into the humid principle; agitated, they exhaled smoke like a fire, and from " their depth arose a plaintive and ineffable sound. Methought I heard the voice " of light [d]. The earth and the water were confused; the earth was not ap- " parent, it was covered with the humid principle; the Spiritual Word moved " above this nature and agitated it."

" Pimander said to me, Understandest thou this vision? The light is myself, thy " God Intellect, more ancient than the humid nature, which shines amidst darknesses, " and the Word, irradiating from the Intellect, is the Son of God. Then I said, What " will be hereafter? *Know that which thou seest and hearest in thyself is the Word* " *of the Lord* [e]; but the Intellect is God the Father, they are not separated, for their " union is life."

Thus, the creation of the world is the image of regeneration; the mind of man is an emanation from God, in whom we live and move and have our being [f]. The

---

[a] Psalm xxxiii. verse 6.

[b] Iohan, xx. verse 22.

[c] Acts of the Apostles, chap. ii.

[d] Hear the voice of fire, said Zoroaster: Κλῦθι πυρὸς τὴν φωνὴν. (Oracula Magica Zoroastri.)

[e] Οὕτω γνῶθι, τὸ ἐν σοὶ βλέπον καὶ ακοῦον, λόγος Κυρίου. (Pimander, cap. i. sect. 6.)

[f] Acts, chap. xvii. verse 28.

Holy Ghost is the bond which unites the creature to the creator. The intellect, adds Hermes, is God androgynous, for he is life and light. As demiurgus, or creator, he produced by his word the other operating mind, which is the God of fire or spirit or breath [a].

Light and heat, symbols of the wisdom and love of God, were the two principles, male and female. The doctrine of Pimander explains why the Egyptian god Kneph, or the Eternal, was androgynous [b]. Jupiter, according to Orpheus, is the husband, and the immortal nymph, Mithras, appears likewise to have had a divinity male and female [c]. According to rabbinical traditions, Adam was created male and female [d]; love and wisdom existed conjointly in him.

The birth of the world, according to Pimander, is in every thing similar to the Genesis of Moses. God creates man by his Word, and regenerates him by his Holy Spirit, who is love and truth, and of which the double symbol is fire and air, and in the language of colours, red and azure. This doctrine prevails in all the Holy Scriptures; forgotten by the Hebrews, who comprehended only the dead letter of the word, it was again brought to light by the Messiah. It likewise formed the basis of the Egyptian theology, and of the hieroglyphs, shewing us its existence on the front of all temples.

" A learned Englishman states, that the Egyptian Triad was represented by a globe, a serpent, and a wing. The globe was an emblem of God, because that his centre is everywhere and his circumference immeasurable; the serpent designates eternity and likewise wisdom; the wing was the symbol of air, or the spirit." [e]

We shall further study the symbol of the serpent, and recognise its indicating the Word, the good serpent Meissi, according to an expression of Horapollo.

On a monument of Thebes, engraved and coloured in the description of Egypt, (Tom. iii. pl. 34. of the French government work,) the globe is red, the two serpents are golden, and the wings red and azured; the interval between the two serpents is filled by a green tint. The red is the symbol of love divine, the gold, or golden yellow, indicates the word, Revelation; the azure the air, or divine breath; the green was the last divine sphere, which is again found in the emerald rainbow of the apocalypse.

[a] Ηνώματος, Pimander, cap. i. sect. 9.
[b] Plutarch, Isis et Osir.
[c] Creuzer, Religions de l'Antiquité, comp. a turre de Mithra, p. 175.
[d] Othonis lexicon rabbinico-phil., verbo Adam.
[e] Vide de Marles, Histoire Générale de l'Inde, t. ii. p. 81, who quotes from the Rev. Thomas Maurice.
—This remarkable symbol will be hereafter discussed, which at present would exceed the limits of a note.

The interpretation of this hieroglyph becomes easy. God, in his unity, which embraces the universe, is love; he reveals himself by wisdom and goodness, signified by the two serpents and gold; he recalls creation to him by truth and love, designated by the two wings and by their colour, red and blue.

Whatever may be established prejudices, I ought here to repeat the opinion of a savant offered merely as a conjecture, but which here acquires a high degree of certainty. "It is Iso, it is Jesus, Saviour of the World and Son of Justice, that the Egyptians figured on all the gates of their temples; and the signification of this symbol was therefore that which Malachi has transmitted (ch. iv. verse 2). Unto you that fear my name shall the Sun of Righteousness arise with healing in his wings."[a]

This approximation will doubtless appear strange to persons who forget that the Messiah is called by the Fathers of the Church, the sun and the good serpent, that the Holy Ghost descended on the anointed of the Lord in the form of a dove; and finally, that the globe, the serpent, and the wings, have precisely the same signification on monuments of the middle ages as on the temples of Thebes[b]. Christians will here perceive confirmation of the prophecies and truth of Christianity; of that divine religion which was announced not only to an isolated class, forgotten by the world, but whose appearance was preceded by the expectation of the universe.

Hieroglyphs reproduce the doctrine of Pimander; sacred legends collected by Greek authors on the Egyptian Triad confirm this tenet, and seal its authenticity.

The Eternal God, the principle of all existence, was revered under the name of Kneph. The inhabitants of the Thebaid, according to Plutarch[c], at first knew no other God, nor worshipped no mortal divinity; afterwards, this religion, like all others, followed a general law, and was absorbed in fetischism. From the mouth of Kneph issued the egg of the world, for God created the universe by his word—from this egg was born the third divine principle, fire, revered under the name of Phtha[d]. Kneph and Phtha were the same divinity adored in its triple essence, under three attributes.

Iamblichus, in his treatise on the mysteries of Egypt, explains this sacred triad. The first principle, guardian of wisdom and of truth, is named Amon, when it is revealed by light, and Phtha, when it achieved creation by fire[e]. This passage is a

---

[a] Lacour, Essai sur les Hiéroglyphes, p. 98. Comp. Junker, des Ailes et des divinités ailées.

[b] The wing is the power of a bird, as the arm is the power of man; the Holy Ghost is the power of God, it had a wing for its symbol.

[c] Plutarch. de Isid. et Osir.

[d] Eusebii Præp. Evang. lib. iii. cap. xi. p. 115.

[e] Iamblichus, de Mysteriis, p. 159.

commentary on this doctrine by Hermes Trismegistus. We remark that Kneph, as the spirit pervading nature, was painted azure colour, and as the Saviour of Man appeared under the form of the serpent Cnuphis, who had a temple in the Elephantine isle [a].

The antique creeds of Persia are identified with the Indian, Egyptian, and Hebrew doctrine; according to Zoroaster, boundless time, the first principle, created primitive light and immaterial fire.

The Word, or the second principle, is the soul of Ormus; he pronounced it, and all pure beings, past, present, and to come, have been created by it; that word is *I am* [b].

Fire is the principle of union between Ormus and the being absorbed into the Highest, he is the life of the soul; under the form of wind he is the breath of Ormus. What was this tenet? The author of the Vendidad-Sadé replies, that he has the prudence not to explain it [c].

The theogony of Sanchoniathon appears formed on the outlines of the doctrines which we exhibit. Desire, or love, is the God creator of the universe. Irradiating from light, he unites himself to darkness. At his voice the air enflames, the lightning shines, the thunder peals, and the animals awake from the sleep of the dead, and move in the earth, the air, and the water [d].

According to Evander, this inscription remains on an Egyptian column :—To the Night, and to the Day, and to the father of all which is and shall be, *to Love* [e]. It is of little consequence whether this column were erected by Egyptians or by Greeks, because other monuments prove that the doctrine of these two people was the same in its principle, though different in form. Orpheus seems to have copied Sanchoniathon, who himself wrote according to the books of Thaut, or Hermes, as related by Philo de Byblos.

The fable of Cupid was a sacred legend, materialized by the Greeks, but which in the sanctuaries long preserved its primitive signification.

Aristophanes said that Night, with black wings, bore an egg, whence love was born [f]. Antiphanes, in his theogony, relates that Cupid, father of light and the gods, emanated from chaos and night [g]. Apuleius reproduced the same doctrine in

[a] Jablonski, lib. i. cap. ix. p. 87; Pantheon Ægyptiorum.
[b] Zent-Avesta.
[c] Vendidad-Sadé, p. 180.
[d] Eusebii Præp. Evang. lib. i. cap. ix.
[e] Jablonski, Pantheon Ægyptiorum, lib. i. cap. i. p. 18.
[f] Aristophanes in Avibus; Jablonski, lib. i. cap. i.
[g] Irenæus contra Hæres, lib. ii. cap. xiv.

his symbolic romance of the Golden Ass. The adventures of Psyche develope the degrees of the regeneration of the soul : divine love, which embraces it ; the temptations which she resists, the proofs that she undergoes, previous to tasting the cup of immortality. The Cupid of India, Câmadêva, the god of desire, confirms this interpretation. One of his epithets is Atmabou, existence of the soul ; his mother is Maya, or the general attractive power ; his attributes are a fish on a red ground. The fish is the symbol of primitive waters, or chaos ; the red colour, that of divine love, presiding at the creation of the soul [a]. Likewise Eros, or the celestial Cupid, according to Plato and Cicero, was son of Jupiter and Venus, i. e. of Initiation, as we shall hereafter prove.

Red colour, designated among the Greeks, as in India and Egypt, Love, the sanctifier and regenerator. The colours attributed to Pan, the Universe, God, establishes the tenet of the divine triad,—his body was white as snow, he had golden horns, emblems of the power of revelation. It is in this relation that he is confounded with the Sun and the light, symbol of the divine manifestation—his hair was red, his countenance fiery. Orpheus sung, I call Pan the great whole, and the fire eternal [b].

CONSECRATED LANGUAGE.

Sacrifices in their original institution were symbols of the love of man for his creator ; the first fruits of harvest and of animals were presented on the altars, emblems of our thoughts and affections [c].

The sacrificial fire in the Jadjour-Veda, is the symbol of the celestial fire which dwells in the heart. In the Sanscrit, different expressions which designate fire have the symbolic signification of the No. 3, *Vahni*, &c. The name of the divinity Om has the same numerical meaning. So in the Thibetian language, Mé signifies fire and the No. 3 [d].

Thus the third divine attribute, or the Holy Ghost the love of God, and worship, have the same symbol, fire, which is translated in the language of colours by red.

A tradition prevalent amongst all nations states, that fire has created and will destroy the world ; for the soul emanating from the love of God must return into

[a] Langlès, notes sur les Recherches Asiatiques, tom. i. p. 272.

[b] Compare Natalis Comilis Myth, lib. v. et Gyraldi Syntad. Deor. XV.

[c] Πυρφορος was synonymous for ignem ferens and triticum ferens.

[d] Asiatic Journal, July, 1835.

his bosom. One of the names of the divinity in Hebrew is that of fire, אש. In the Indian mythology, Siva is the fire which created the world, and which must consume it. Orpheus reproduces the same dogma that Egypt represented by the phœnix—(phœnim the cherubim?).

Fire, the symbol of the purification and regeneration of the soul, explains the custom of burning the bodies of the dead, the barbarous superstition which constrains Hindu widows to consume themselves on their husband's funeral pile, and the fanaticism of the Gymnosophists, who condemned themselves to this punishment to gain heaven, according to Strabo.

In China, red colour is consecrated to religion [a], and the mourning worn by children is hempen sackcloth of a bright red [b]. Love always had a red colour for the symbol of infancy. Cupid is a child; celestial love is represented in Christian symbolism by infant angels. A child was initiated into the great mysteries at Eleusis; he performed a character in the last initiation, which was an emblem of death; he was named the child of the sanctuary [c]; and the boys of the choir are to this day clothed in red. Love is a stranger to all but innocent and pure hearts. The kingdom of heaven, said Jesus Christ, is inherited by those who are like little children. In pagan antiquity, red was the symbol of innocence and of virginity; the mystic couches used in the mysteries of Eleusis, bound round with purple fillets, designate the virginity of Proserpine when she arrived at hell [d].

Xenophon describes a Persian ceremony, testifying the tenet of the divine triad and its triple symbol, white, gold, and red. Amidst an immense procession are three chariots; the first was white, crowned with flowers, with the pole gilt, an offering to the supreme god; the second chariot, of the same colour and similarly decorated, was consecrated to the sun; the horses of the third chariot were caparisoned with scarlet housings, behind which marched men bearing the sacred fire [e]. The first and second cars were similar, and in the Persian doctrine, as in the Pimander, the Supreme Being is identified with the Word. It would be easy to multiply examples demonstrating that love, fire, and red colour, were synonymous in the language of symbols; it still remains in the fires annually lighted in the provinces on the vigil of St. John, in memorial of the baptism by fire [f].

---

[a] Visdelou, Notice sur l'Y-King à la Suite du Chou-King, p. 428.

[b] Prevost, Histoire générale des Voyages, tom. vi. p. 155.

[c] Probably the origin of the boy bishop at Salisbury, &c.

[d] Sainte-Croix, Mystères du Paganism, tom. i. p. 320.

[e] Xenophon, Cyrop. lib. iii.

[f] In Christian symbolism, St. Paul represents love by deeds, as St. Peter truth and faith.

The architecture of antique temples presents additional applications of these principles. The name and form given to the pyramids [a], or columns of fire, used as tombs by the kings of Egypt, are not the effect of fancy or chance. The obelisks, symbols of Amon, the divine word, were not placed as a vain ornament at the entry of temples [b].

Languages, likewise, may have similar tendency. The genitive, which designates generation, is formed in the grammar of almost every people by a termination which in primitive idioms, as Hebrew, signifies fire, *as, es, is,* or only *s*. From thence the name of divinities, considered in their attributes of love, is formed by these syllables. The *ases* is again found among the Scandinavians, by an opposition which we have proved in each symbol. The *asours* amongst the Indians are the evil genii.

In Etruscan language, *eso* was the epithet of Jupiter, *esu* signifies being, *esuk,* and *esou,* or *æsar,* according to Suetonius, God [c]. We again find the same etymology in Vesta, the goddess of sacred fire, in the words *æstus,* heat, *æstas,* or *esté,* according to ancient orthography, the summer. Jesus, is he not the god of love invoked by the faithful, as well as Christ, the name pronounced by the unbiassed understanding [d]?

The necessary consequence of these facts is, that the language of colours ought to adopt them by giving red costumes to all these divinities as attributes of love.

Jehovah appeared to Moses in the midst of a burning bush; a column of fire guided the Israelites in the desert; the lightning shone, the thunder rolled, and the Eternal, surrounded by a flaming fire, descended on Mount Sinai, as in the smoke of a furnace [e]. The throne of God, said the prophet Daniel, was "like the fiery flame, "and his wheels as burning fire, a fiery stream issued and came forth from before "him." [f]

This symbol of love divine revealing itself to man is again found in pagan religions. Vischnou, says the Bagavadam, appeared at first in the human form, with a body clothed with purple and brighter than the sun, similar to the fire which is

---

[a] Pyr-omed, edifice dedicated to fire.

[b] The obelisk represents the ray of light. (Nestor l'Hôte, Notice sur les Obélisques, p. 5.) In the figurative characters described by Champollion, the obelisk is the symbol of Amon.

[c] Passeri picturæ Etruscorum, iii. pl. 131.

[d] According to Swedenborg, (*Arcana cœlestia,* 3004 to 3011,) the name of Jesus relates to divine love, and the name of Christ to divine wisdom.

[e] Exodus, xix, &c., ante.

[f] Daniel, vii. 9, 10.

found in wood, in stones, in the water, and in air [a]. Vischnou is everywhere [b]. This divinity is the Demiurgus, who created the world in his love. Brahma is the regenerator of souls, he is the divine breath, the Spirit of God floating above the primitive waters. In the fulness of time the universe returned into the bosom of Vischnou. This god, absorbed in the repose of a contemplative reverie, rested on the serpent Atisechen, and floated on a sea of milk; destiny made a lotus stalk issue from his navel, the flower expanded itself to the rays of the divine sun, which is Vischnou himself; he said, Arise, O Brahma! and a spirit, the colour of flame, appeared, having four heads and four hands, symbols of the four vedas [c].

Red colour was consecrated in Egypt to good genii, as we perceive afterward the Greek Jupiter was called *Zeus*, life, heat, fire, and according to Winkelmann, he is clothed in red [d]. The blue mantle was equally consecrated to him, a crown of flames ornamented his head, and the eagle, with wings extended, rested at his feet. On a monument described by Junker, the body of Jupiter is surrounded by a serpent, marked with the twelve signs of the zodiac [e]. This serpent, symbol of the sun's course, was the hieroglyph of the Word. Thus in Greece, as in Egypt and in Christianity, the Trinity was represented by the red globe, or the crown of flames, by wings, and by the serpent.

Jupiter appears identified with the Indian god Vischnou. Fire, which creates and animates the universe, is the symbol of these two divinities. Do we not find the same analogy between Brahma and Bacchus, nourished, according to Eustathius, on mount Merou, the sacred mountain of the Indians? Brahma and Bacchus are symbols of divine love, which regenerates souls, of the baptism by fire, and of sanctification. A passage of Olympiodorus removes all doubts in this respect as to the Grecian divinity, "The object of the mysteries is to lead back the soul to its principle, to its primitive and final state, i. e. life in Jupiter, whence it descended with Bacchus, who will conduct it back again." [f]

Bacchus is the regenerator and civilizer of mankind; he bestows moral force, as its emblem, wine, gives vigour to the material body. The god of wine, in his last materialization, preserves his primitive symbol, the red colour. In two pictures, the

---

[a] Electricity—termed a *modern* discovery.

[b] Bagavadam, p. 11.

[c] Vide the Bagavadam, p. 62, and extract from the Shaster, in the preliminary discourse of Bhaguat-Geeta, p. 118.

[d] Winckelmann, Histoire de l'Art, tom. ii. p. 187.

[e] Junker, on the mode of representing the Eternal Father according to the Greeks, pp. 351—353.

[f] Extrait d'un Commentaire d'Olympiodore sur le Phedon, Journal des Savans, Mars 1835.

one described by Philostratus, the other from the collection of Herculaneum, Bacchus is clothed with a red mantle[a].

However, I ought not to omit that this colour, according to Plutarch, was consecrated to all divinities[b]. On their festival days their statues were coloured with red, and minium was put on their cheeks[c]. Love! is it not the basis of all worship, even in its last degradation?

Christianity restored truth to mankind, and reinstated symbolic language in its original purity. In the transfiguration the countenance of our Lord became resplendent as the sun, and his vesture shone like the light. Such, in their highest energy, are the symbols of divine love and wisdom. The angel who rolled away the stone from the sepulchre reproduced them in an inferior order; his face shone like lightning, and his robe was white as snow[d]. Finally, in the last degree appeared the Just, in robes washed white in the blood of the Lamb[e].

The artists of the middle ages preserved these precious traditions, and gave to Jesus Christ after the resurrection[f], white or red costume.

Red colour being established as a symbol of the divinity, and consecrated to his worship, we proceed to its application in the costume of pontiffs and kings.

Purple and scarlet, coloured the ephod and breastplate of Aaron[g]. The general signification of these two colours indicates the love of God, their different gradations of colour manifest the varieties of this love. We shall state these differences in the description of the hyacinth colour.

The sovereign pontiff of Hieropolis only had the right to wear a robe of purple, the priests were clothed in white[h].

In the mysteries of Eleusis, the priests wore long robes of purple. The mystic, or candidate for the mysteries of Samothrace, presented himself crowned with branches of the olive and with a veil of purple colour, of which it was related Ulysses used the first; before him it was customary only to use narrow fillets of the same colour[i].

---

[a] Creuzer, Religions de l'Antiquité, i. 65.

[b] Plutarch. Quæst. Roman. 98.

[c] Court de Gebelin, Monde primitif, viii. 203.

[d] St. Matthew, xvii. 2; xxviii. 3.

[e] Apocalypse.

[f] Guigniaut, on the Symbolism of Creuzer, i. p. 552. The red and the white are the two colours consecrated to Jehovah, as the god of love and of wisdom, in numerous miniatures and illuminations.

[g] Exodus, ch. xxviii.

[h] Lucianus de Dea Syria, p. 483.

[i] St. Croix, Mysterès du Paganism, tom. i. pp. 52, 231. and 286.

The middle ages attached the same symbolic ideas to red colour; the costume of priests reproduced it, and it is again found on banners. Eusebius describes the labarum, or standard of Constantine, which he saw; it was a cross, whence depended a square ensign of a very precious purple stuff[a]. The Oriflamme, according to popular legends, was sent from heaven to Clovis, its colour was purple azured. Wendelin ascertained that the Oriflamme was the banner of the monks of St. Denis. The French Dionysius bears the name of the Greek Bacchus, Dionusos; the symbolic signification of this divinity is the same as that of the banner of the ancient kings of France[b], i. e. sanctification. At the festival of the Saint-Esprit, the Roman Catholic priest wears red ornaments, and the altar consecrated to the Holy Ghost is decorated with this colour.

Among the Arabs, red was the symbol of religious duties. Mahomet wore red robes on Friday, and the festival of Beyram[c].

In antiquity, the ruby was the popular emblem of happiness. If it changed its colour it was a sinister presage, but it again took its purpled tint when the misfortune was past. It banished sadness and repressed luxury; it resisted poison, preserved from the plague, and dispelled evil thoughts. The materialization of the symbol of divine love is here plainly discerned. In Eastern tales, the carbuncle shines in darkness, and expands its light afar. Lucian describes a similar stone (De Syria Dea, p. 478). The ancients consecrated the carbuncle to the sun. (Caussin, Symb. p. 617.)

The purple mantle of kings was the emblem of the power of God, or right divine.

According to Josephus, the costume of the kings of Egypt was of a purple colour; it was the same amongst the most ancient Greeks. In the Vatican Library is a copy of an antique painting, representing Minerva holding a purple fillet, designating the sovereignty which she offers Paris in exchange for the apple[d]. The appropriation of this colour to royalty was universal amongst ancient nations[e].

" Red (Court de Gebelin) was in Rome the colour for generals, the nobility, and

[a] Eusebii de Vitâ Constan. lib. i. c. 28.

[b] Azure purple, the colour of the Oriflamme, united the two colours assigned to the Holy Ghost, red and blue, and represents the union of love and truth in God. We perceive that the myth of Bacchus, and the colour appropriated to this divinity, designate divine love; and in the Bible, wine is the symbol of celestial truth.

[c] Mouradja d'Hosson, tom. iv. 1re part. p. 162.

[d] Compare André Lens, Costumes de l'Antiquité, pp. 15 and 71.

[e] Amati de restitutione purpurarum, p. 75, et passim.

patricians; consequently it became that of the emperors. Those of Constantinople were clothed entirely in red. Thus the last of the princes, being overwhelmed in the crowd, fighting valiantly against the Turks, who captured his capital, he was recognised by his red boots amidst a mountain of the slain.

" Their edicts, their signature, their seals, were in red ink and wax. Gules was borne for their arms, which was the origin of the laws forbidding any but princes thus to use it.

" The clavus, the distinguishing ornament of patricians at Rome, which being broader or narrower, forms the laticlavium or the angusti-clavium, was a purple band, similar to a border of studs, those consecrated nails, which assured the duration of the republic, and were fixed every year."[*]

The right of the Roman patricians to wear purple was of sacred origin; each father of a family was formerly king and pontiff. The development of this historical fact would too much extend this essay; let us only recollect the barbarity of the Justinian code, which condemned to death the buyer and seller of a purple stuff.

Cardinals now inherit this symbol of sovereignty.

According to the twofold import of colours, the sinister symbol of divine love will indicate hatred, egotism, and infernal love, the devil will appear clothed in red, and the fires of sacrifices will be contrasted by those of hell.

So, according to the prophet, God is surrounded by the fire which animates the heart for noble passions, hell will appear as a fierce furnace, from whence will exhale the heat of wrath, of envy, and all crimes and vices. The condemned, doomed to eternal fire, submit to the rule of their evil passions; the flame which devours them is not without, but within their hearts.

Jeremiah said of false prophets, that they are clothed in hyacinth and purple. We shall see that these combinations of red and of blue, reproduce the dualism of love and of truth in a particular meaning. The prophet signifies by these colours evil and error, in opposition to the true sages, who are the good and the true.

It is in the same sense that Isaiah (i. 18.) said, " Though your sins be as scarlet they shall be as white as snow; though they be red like crimson, they shall be as wool." Everywhere in the Bible the same dual of the good and the true is exhibited in opposition to evil and error.

By comparing symbols, the signification which should be given to each is readily ascertained. There are in this consecrated language, no rules other than in popular

* Monde primitif, tom. viii. p. 202.— The words of the wise, said Solomon, are as nails fastened by the masters of assemblies. (Ecclesiastes, xii. 11.) Yet the nail head moulding is usually considered an ornament of NORMAN Architecture.

idioms, in which words are often understood to mean good or bad, accordingly as they are placed. For example, the parable of the rich man and Lazarus, in St. Luke, 16th chapter. The Evangelist addresses himself to the spiritual man, not to the material; every word possesses a spiritual signification. The rich man is he who has much intellectual knowledge, good or evil. The kingdom of heaven does not belong necessarily to those who die of hunger, and hell is not an heritage entailed to the powerful of the earth; but the poor in spirit will be accepted by God, whilst the proud boaster excludes himself. Lazarus is the poor in spirit. This rich man is not the falsely wise depicted by Jeremiah, but the man possessing the knowledge of God. This man is the Jewish nation, clothed in purple and fine linen, symbols of love and wisdom, or of knowledge of the good and the true. Lazarus represents the Gentiles, who, yet unknowing them, desire and claim those spiritual riches which they will enjoy in another life.

Painters of the middle ages likewise attribute an infernal signification to red colour; numerous applications are extant in miniatures and large church windows.

Blazonry preserves its double signification. The gules, or red, in coats of arms, observes La Colombière, denotes in spiritual virtues, ardent love towards God and one's neighbour; in mundane virtues, valour and energy; in vice, cruelty, wrath, murder, and carnage; of the four elements, fire; in the complexions of men, the choleric; in precious stones, the ruby. It represents the day of judgment, because it is believed that the world will be consumed by fire. (Science héroïque, p. 36.)

Red, like white, was also a mortuary colour, and appears to have been equally consecrated to good and to evil, to the celestial as to the infernal deities.

The priests and priestesses of Eleusis pronounced their imprecations against Alcibiades upstanding and turning to the west, and shaking their purple robes. In sacrificing to the Eumenides, it was obligatory to wear robes of this colour. Wrought wool, tinted purple, ought likewise to be used in the sacrifices preparatory to the mysteries. The couches of the initiated, during the celebration of the festival of Ceres, were bound round by narrow fillets of the same colour. Homer gives to the dead the epithet, *purpurea*; and Artemidorus says that purple colour is assigned to death. "Those who have lived piously ought to live in elysium, in fields enamelled with purple roses. The ancients strewed on the tombs flowers of purple and saffron . . . All these customs were allegorical, and related to the future life; for the initiated were considered as having passed through the state of death, whence arose the conformity of several ceremonies of initiation with those which were used in sepulchres and funereal sacrifices."[a]

During the middle ages, red was a mortuary colour; some miniatures in the Salisbury breviary show biers covered with red palls[b]. In this example, was it an emblem of virginity and innocence, as in Greece and China, or was it only a token of honour to the remains of kings or cardinals?

PROFANE OR POPULAR LANGUAGE.

In the popular language of every nation, the colour of blood, red, was the emblem of combat; in Peru, the quipos, tinted red, designated warriors[c]. The Spartans were shrouded in red winding sheets. This colour was appropriate for the funerals of a people who existed by war, and had no other than military courage. The god Mars had red colour for his attribute; but here, materialized in popular opinions, the symbol had another meaning for the priests;—the god of war for the profane, was the god of spiritual combats for the initiated. The learned Creuzer remarks, that Homer enables us to perceive in this divinity the god of nature performing the great work of cosmic generation and organization.[d]. The identity of the Egyptian god Phtha and the Grecian Hephaistos (Vulcanus, ignis) demonstrates it.

Initiation prefigured the regeneration of man by the generation of nature. Man was the microcosm, the little world, which must be spiritually born by the combat of divine love against human passions. Jehovah, does he not say that He is the God of armies and of combats? Jesus, does he not say that He comes to create war? In numerous MSS. of the thirteenth and fourteenth centuries, King David appears in an ecstacy before an angel, whose body, wings, vesture and drawn sword are of a bright red; these are signs of divine love animating the prophet king in the name of the God of spiritual combats[e].

Red colour (of blood) was the emblem of shame in the countenance[f] in the

---

[a] St. Croix, Mystères du Paganism, tom. i. p. 286.
[b] Breviarium Sarisbur.; MSS. de la Bibliothèque Royale, 15me siècle.
[c] Garcillasso de la Vega, Histoire des Incas, tom. ii. p. 285.
[d] Creuzer, Religions de l'Antiquité, liv. vii. chap. iv. p. 644.
[e] Emblèmes bibliques du 14me siècle, MSS. de la Biblioth. Royale, No. 6829.
[f] Rerum Alamannicarum Scriptores ex Bibl. Goldasti, tom. i. p. 126.

middle ages. Diogenes named red the colour of virtue, doubtless for the same reason[a]. In its last popular expression it became the emblem of crime expiated on the scaffold. The executioner, born to shed blood, is generally habited in red, or else in yellow[b], the choice of one of these two colours being imperative on him.

OF BLUE.

DIVINE LANGUAGE.

The air is in the Bible the symbol of the Holy Spirit, of the divine truth which enlightens mankind. The miracle on the day of Pentecost, (Acts, ii.,) when the apostles " were all filled with the Holy Ghost," describes it as " a mighty rushing wind, with cloven tongues like as of fire." In the Gospel of St. John, 3rd chapter, 8th verse, the Redeemer says, " The wind bloweth where it listeth, and thou hearest the sound thereof, but canst not tell whence it cometh, and whither it goeth ; so is every one that is born of the Spirit."

The Holy Ghost is God in us as love and as truth ; these two attributes reunited had the dove for a symbol. When Jesus was baptized, John saw the Spirit of God descending on him as a dove. The symbol of the Spirit is air, even so is its colour, azure, or celestial blue. In Christian theology, the Holy Ghost proceeds from the Father and the Son. God is love, Christ is truth ; their symbols are red and azure, the Holy Ghost proceeding from these two was represented by red and blue.

Antiquity typified this dogma by the ethereal fire. In Hindhustan is found the god of fire, Agni (Ignis), with two faces, symbols of the fire terrestrial and fire celestial ; he rides on a ram of azure colour, with red horns[c].

We find Jupiter Ammon with similar attributes, represented of a blue colour, with rams' horns.

In oriental languages, the word *azur* signifies fire, and in blazonry it designates blue colour.

Jupiter Axur, or Auxur[d], explains this double signification. According to the Greeks, says St. Clement, the ethereal fire is their god Zeus (Jupiter). He is made the supreme god because of his igneous nature[e]. The fragments of Pherecydes

[a] La Mothe-le-Vayer, Opuscules, p. 246.
[b] Ibid. p. 250.
[c] Langlès, Monum. de l'Hindoustan, tom. i. p. 191.
[d] Ibid. p. 176.
[e] Homil. VI. Comp. Emeric David, Jupiter, introd. p. xxvi.

attest this dogma[a]. The ethereal fire, or red and blue reunited, typify the identification of love and wisdom in the father of gods and men. We shall see this
symbol represented and developed on Christian monuments by the violet colour.

In cosmogonies, divine wisdom creates the world, God, the creator, is always
coloured blue. Vischnou, according to the sacred books of Hindhustan, was born
of a blue colour[b]. Does not this indicate that wisdom emanated from God is symbolized by azure? On Langlès' Indian Monuments, Vischnou is twice represented
creating the world—his body is celestial blue.

In Egypt, the Supreme God, the creator of the universe, Cneph, was painted
sky blue[c]. In Greece, azure is the colour of Jupiter. In China, heaven is the
supreme god; and in Christian symbolism, the azured vault is the mantle which
veils the divinity. Azure is likewise the symbol of God the Saviour, redeemer of
mankind.

The Indian god Vischnou is the divine sun, the eternal mind, the word of God.
He is the chief preserver, the divine wisdom, which is self-incarnate in the person of
Krichna to save mankind. He was born (Bagavadam, p. 276) with a black spot
on his breast; he appeared covered with royal purple, celestial blue was the colour of
his body, whence is derived the name, Krichna, or Crisnen. This remarkable incarnation represents the Supreme Being, in the fulness of his divinty, descended on
earth[d]. The legend of Krichna very much resembles the life of Christ;—the birth
in a stable, the massacre of the infants, are found in the Bagavadam; but not only
the Evangelists but the Apocalypse is paraphrased in the religious traditions of
Hindhustan. "The Messiah is not expected by the Jews with more certainty and
" impatience than the tenth incarnation of Vischnou (Kalki Avatara) by the too
" credulous Hindhus. Every day they expect to see Vischnou appear on horseback,
" armed with a scimetar, shining like a comet; he will come to terminate the present
" age (Kali-Youga), and commence an age of purity and virtue. Thus the Hindoos,
" like most other nations, have the prophetic tradition of a Redeemer, and par-
" ticularly of a future judge. This horse, named Kalki, involuntarily reminds us of
" the white horse mentioned in the Apocalypse."[e]

Identical symbols reappear in Egypt. Amon is the divine word, the new sun,
the sun of spring. He enters the golden circle of the year by appearing in the sign

[a] Pherecyd. Fragm. pp. 44, 45.

[b] Extrait du Shaster, discours préliminaire du Bhaguat-Geeta, p. 114.

[c] Noël, verbo Cneph, Court de Gebelin, tom. viii. p. 202.

[d] Crishna was the person of Vischnou himself in a human form.—Sir Wm. Jones, vol. iii. p. 375.

[e] Langlès, Monumens de l'Hindoustan, tom. i. p. 188.

Aries; victor over the darkness of the inferior hemisphere, he expands his heat and light upon the earth [a]. His image, according to Eusebius, was that of a man sitting, of an azure colour, with a ram's head [b]; he is thus represented on Egyptian paintings [c].

The Fathers of the Church call Jesus the new sun, the lamb divine, sacrificed to efface the sins of the world and to conquer the spirit of darkness. On paintings of the middle ages, the robe of the Messiah is blue during the three years of his preaching truth and wisdom.

CONSECRATED LANGUAGE.

Symbolism distinguishes three blue colours; one which emanates from red, another from white, and a third allied to black, frequently distinguished by different gradations of colour, and sometimes confounded in one alone.

The blue emanated from red represents the ethereal fire; its signification is the *celestial love of truth*. In the mysteries, it relates to the baptism by fire.

The blue emanated from white indicates the truth of faith; it relates to the living waters of the Bible, or to the baptism of the Spirit.

The blue allied to black conducts us back to the cosmogony, to the Spirit of God moving on chaos; it relates to natural baptism.

These three aspects of the same colour correspond to the three principal degrees of antient initiation, and to the triple baptism of Christianity. St. John said, I baptize with water, to lead you to repentance, but He who cometh after me is mightier than I, He will baptize you with the Holy Ghost and with fire. These three degrees are particularized in painting by red, blue, and green. Green, black, and deep blue, indicate the world born from the depth of the primitive waters, and the first degree of initiation. Azure represents regeneration, or the spiritual formation of man, and red the sanctification.

[a] Jablonski, Pantheon, lib. ii. cap. 2.

[b] Praeparat. Evang. lib. iii. cap. 12.

[c] In the mystic chamber of the temple of Philæ, by the First Cataract, is *Amun-Kneph* turning a potter's wheel with his foot, and moulding with his hands, out of a lump of clay, Osiris, the father of men. Amun-Kneph, or Neph, Kneph, Chnouphis, Noub, Khnem, Knem, represents the "creative power of Amun," i. e. the "Spirit of God," the breath of life, breathed into the nostrils of the first created man. The translation of the hieroglyphic inscription above the figure is, "Khnem, the creator, on his wheel, moulds the divine members of Osiris in the shining house of life."—Vide Champollion le Jeune, and compare Isaiah, chap. lxiv. verse 8.

When Vischnou, the supreme god of the Indians, represents the last degree of regeneration, he is of a deep blue, or verditer colour. According to Paulin de St. Barthélemy, the ancients confounded deep blue colour with green, and also with black [a].

Saturn as Memnon, as Osiris-Serapis; as Kneph-Ammon-Agathodemon-Nilus; as Vischnou-Narayana, Krichna, Bouddha, was black, or deep blue, and according to Guigniaut, all these deities have some relation to water [b].

Krichna, as the incarnation of truth divine, is coloured azure; but abased to humanity, he is subjected to the temptations of evil, and Indian symbolism equally consecrates deep blue and black to him [c].

Plutarch (in Iside) states Osiris to be of a black colour, because water blackens substances which it saturates; from this the primitive idea of God agitating chaos is evident.

The statue of Saturn in his temple was of black stone. His priests were Ethiopians, Abyssinians, or from other black nations; they wore blue vestments and rings of iron. When the king entered this temple, his suite wore blue or black [d].

The opposition of these two colours represents the antagonism of life and death, in the spiritual and material states, manifested in the age of which Saturn is the symbol.

The temple and statue of Mercury were of blue stones; one of his arms was white, the other black. (Gœrres, i. 295.) Macrobius assigns him one wing white, the other blue, or black, according to some mythographers. White plumes open the gates of heaven, and black, those of hell;—a black and white mantle was also given him [e]. Blue colour, associated with black, is the attribute of the initiator destroying the gates of spiritual death by the power of truth. White typifies perfect regeneration, passing the celestial precincts.

Blue-black was the colour which the Greeks named Cyanine (Κύανος). A sacred legend gives this fable a dramatic form. Between Europe and Asia, at the entrance of the Hellespont, rise two rocks; the waves beat furiously on them, and throw up vapours, obscuring the air. These are the Cyanine rocks. The Argonauts, frightened at their appearance, let loose a dove, which passed them safely; the dove

---

[a] Paulin: Musei Borgiani Codices, pp. 63—201.

[b] Notes sur la Symbolique de Creuzer, tom. i. p. 548.

[c] Sir W. Jones on gods of Greece, vol. iii. p. 377. Paulin. Systema Brahmanicam, p. 146.

[d] Gœrres Mythengeschichte der Asiatischen Welt i. 299.

[e] Noël, Dictionnaire de la Fable, verbo Mercure.—The modern Egyptians term dark blue, black (vide Lane). When the conjuror's boy sees the figure of Lord Nelson, he describes the naval uniform as black.

is the symbol of divine love. These navigators offered sacrifices to Juno, who gave them calm weather. Juno is the air, symbol of celestial truth. They also sacrificed to Neptune, who stayed these moveable rocks. Neptune, or water, represents natural truth; thus regenerated man cannot avoid the shoals of the false and the true, but by entering through the three degrees of the love of God, of spiritual truths, and of their application to worldly intercourse; which are the indestructible bases of all regeneration.

Neptune had green drapery; black bulls were sacrificed to him [a]. Blue colour was consecrated to Juno [b].

The Messiah wore blue (azure) during his ministry, but black vesture when he combated temptations [c]. Byzantine paintings, attributed to St. Luke, represent the Virgin with a black complexion. In more modern pictures, she has black or bistre drapery; for Jesus descended on earth, inherited from his mother the infirmities of humanity [d].

Azure, in its absolute signification, represents truth divine.

Azure was the symbol of divine eternity, of human immortality, and by a natural consequence became a mortuary colour.

The grand priest of Egypt wore a sapphire on his breast. This image, says Ælian, is named the truth [e].

In the mysteries he wore a celestial blue robe, embroidered with stars all over, and bound by a yellow belt (Montfaucon). These ornaments are seen on the breast-plate of Aaron and his hyacinth robe.

---

[a] Vide the colours, green and black.

[b] Ἥρα δὲ ἀήρ. Compare Lydus de Mensibus, Winkelmann, ii. 187. Guigniaut sur Creuzer, i. 550. 551.

[c] Emblemata Biblica, MSS. of the thirteenth century. Bibliothèque Royale, No. 37.

[d] According to the Chinese philosopher, Lao-Tseu:—"The Tao is the principle of heaven and earth. "The two modes of being of Tao are his inapprehensible nature, and his phenomenal corporal nature; "together called incomprehensibles, or blues present, blues past, and blues future, or incomprehensibles to "the last degree."

"Blue," adds a Chinese commentator, "is a colour formed of black and of red, mixed together to form "a single colour." (Here, again, is the symbol of cosmogony in the union of Love and Erebus, who, "according to Hesiod, gave birth to Æther.) "The colour of heaven is blue; it is the *In* and the *Jang* "reunited in one, i. e. the active and passive principle, the male and female, the obscure and brilliant. All "corporeal beings are produced by inapprehensible nature, emanated from Tao, blue, and blue is the origin "of all subtile natures," &c.— Paulthier on the Tao-te-King Philosophy of the Hindhus, by Colebrooke.

[e] Καὶ ἐκαλεῖτο τὸ ἄγαλμα Ἀλήθεια.— Æliani varia Hist. xiv. 34. The Jews term the Bible Sepher.

The costume of sovereign pontiffs designates them as guardians of eternal truth. In Egyptian tombs many small blue figures and amulets are found.

The Pythagoreans say, that ether, or uranus, was intellect, or the monad. After death, the soul, casting off its material body, darted into boundless ether. Hierocles affirms, that thus appears Truth regeneratrix[a]. In China, blue is attributed to the dead; red designates the living. Red represents fire, vivifying heat; blue, the symbol of the soul after death[b].

In Christian symbolism, azure is similar. In a MS. of the tenth century[c], Jesus, in the tomb, is bound by blue fillets, his countenance is blue, the sepulchre red. Two angels appear on a stone, the one on the right has a blue aureola and violet mantle, symbols of the passion[d] and of the death of Christ. The angel on the left has a yellow aureola and purple mantle, symbol of the triumph of divine love and of revelation.

The Salisbury Breviary contains several miniatures, in which appear biers covered with a blue mortuary cloth. On some others, but more rarely, the pall is red; finally, on one only is the pall red, and the dais which covers the catafalque blue. These two colours, one over the other, indicate divine love raising the soul to immortality. The dais is the emblem of heaven; violet, composed of red and blue, was likewise a mortuary colour. In the same MS. appears a coffin, with a violet pall.

According to Mr. Mone, the Virgin, after the death of Christ, often appears in blue vestures. Thence, adds M. Guigniaut, (sur Creuzer, i. 552,) the priest likewise wears blue during the celebration of the sacred mysteries of Lent, and at the approach of the holy week the images of Christ are veiled with blue.

In these ceremonies is visible the first degree of materialization, the symbol of divine eternity and of human immortality becomes the emblem of carnal death.

Blue colour, says La Mothe-le-Vayer, (Opuscules, p. 245,) throughout the Levant is considered mortuary; nothing but blue is worn as mourning, none dare appear before royalty in this sad livery, and for the same reason, never in such presence is pronounced the grievous word, death.

These customs evince the symbol completely materialized.

a Aurea carmina, p. 213. Ed. Londini.
b Preface of Chou-King, p. xxii.
c Latin Bible of the tenth century, MSS.   Bibliothèque Royale, No. 6, tom. i.
d Vide violet colour.

PROFANE LANGUAGE.

The colour of the celestial dome, azure, was in divine language the symbol of eternal truth; in consecrated language, of immortality; and in profane language, of fidelity.

The beetle in blue stone ornamented the rings of Egyptian warriors. These rings were symbols of the oath of fidelity taken by the soldiers. According to Horus Apollo (p. 13. Ed. Caussin), the scarabeus was the symbol of virility. The ring with this effigy worn by the military, signified that they should be manly, i. e. that they should be faithful to their oath [a].

In blazonry, blue signifies chastity, loyalty, fidelity, and good reputation [b].

Thus from the tenet of eternal wisdom, man passes to the contemplation of his immortality; the tenet is forgotten, the symbol materialized, and now only signifies fidelity [c].

OF BLACK.

White being the symbol of absolute truth, black should be that of error, of annihilation, of that which is not. God alone possesses self-existence; the world is an emanation from him. White reflects all luminous rays. Black is the negation of light, it was attributed to the author of all evil and falsehood [d].

Genesis and the cosmogonies mention the antagonism of light and darkness. The form of this fable varies according to each nation, but the foundation is everywhere the same;—under the symbol of the creation of the world it presents the picture of regeneration and initiation.

To die, says Plutarch, is to be initiated into the great mysteries [e]. A passage in Themistius, cited by Stobeus [f], likewise states the mysteries were the image of life and death. In Egypt, as elsewhere, these took place in the night [g]. In the Isiacs,

[a] Vide Æliani de Animalibus, lib. x. cap. 15, and Caussin. Symb. Egypt. p. 179, and Temple of Fortuna Virilis at Rome.

[b] Anselme, Palais de l'Honneur, p. 11.

[c] "True blue for ever," popular English motto.

[d] The symbolism of colours recognises two blacks, the one opposed to white, or divine truth, the other opposed to red, or to divine love. Painting represents the latter by tan colour, or sombre or rusty red.

[e] St. Croix, Mystères du Paganisme, i. 380.

[f] Serm. 119, p. 104.

[g] St. Croix, tom. ii. p. 161.

the recipiendary was first conducted to the bath, and purified by certain ablutions ; after ten days' probation, he was introduced by the priest into the adytum of the sanctuary. I have approached the confines of death, said Apuleius, having crossed the threshold of Proserpine ; I have repassed all the elements ; at midnight, the sun appeared to me shining with a brilliant light.

The initiated, by becoming regenerate, dies to all carnal passions. The baptismal waters signify the temptations, or spiritual combats, against falsehood and evil, struggles which precede all regeneration. Baptism took place in the night, because it represented the primitive and dark waters which gave birth to the world. Thus the moral creation of the neophyte had its emblem in the creation of the universe.

In China, black is the symbol of the north, of winter, and of water [a]. Homer gives the epithet, black, to the sea [b]. The spiritual struggle, to which every regenerated mortal was subjected, is narrated in the wars of the gods and the giants. Jupiter could not conquer the children of darkness without the assistance of Hercules. This hero was the emblem of the neophyte, as his twelve labours typify perfect regeneration.

The divinity invoked by the mystic was moral beauty, at first clothed in a mourning robe, but soon reinvested with the most brilliant vesture.

In Egypt it is the dark Isis and the dark Athor, having, like the Grecian Venus, the dove for an emblem [c]. In Greece it is Aphrodite Melenis, or the black Venus. Athor was the passive principle, the symbol of chaos and night, which enveloped nature before the creation. Orpheus, or Onomacritos, who borrowed his inspirations from the traditions of Egypt, said, I sing the night, the mother of gods and men— the night, origin of all created things, and we name her Venus [d].

The Abbé Batteaux remarked, that in Oriental languages, *ven*, or *ben*, signifies to blow [e]. The breath of God reposed on chaos, and the dark Venus gave birth to love, the principle of all being. Venus, the symbol of divine love and moral beauty, became in its materialized expression, the goddess who presides over love and marriage. Why, said Plutarch, (Roman Questions,) does the husband first approach his espoused in the night ? The traditions of Venus and the creation of the world give the explanation.

---

[a] Visdelou, Notice sur l'Y-King à la Suite du Chou-King.

[b] Phurnuti de Neptuno.

[c] Creuzer, Religions de l'Antiquité, liv. vi. chap. v. p. 655.

[d] Apuleius confirms this—Elementorum origo initialis . . . Orbis totius alma Venus. (Metamorph. lib. iv.)

[e] Histoire des Causes Premières.—In Arabic, *ben* signifies children, or tribes.

At Phigalia, in Arcadia, is seen (Pausanias, viii. 42) a statue of Ceres, with the head and mane of a horse, in which serpents and other monsters are intertwined. She holds a dolphin in her right hand, and a dove in her left; her body is covered with a black tunic. The horse was consecrated to Neptune. (Creuzer, liv. vi. p. 680.) It indicates here the understanding of man about to be regenerated, but which is still exposed to the evils and falsehood of life; and the black tunic similarizes the temptations and death. The dolphin represents the first degree of initiation, exterior ablution, and the dove, the baptism of truth and love.

Black being the emblem of all that is false and evil, how can this colour be consecrated to divinities of the true and the good? Why, in India, is Crichna the most beautiful of the gods, and Isis and Osiris, the benefactors of Egypt, black?[a] The only answer is, that the beneficent deities descend into the kingdom of darkness to regenerate and regain mankind.

In Egyptian sacrifices, if the priests discovered a single black hair on the victim, it was reputed unclean[b]. Leviticus orders the Israelites to offer only spotless holocausts to the eternal. The material sacrifice was an emblem of the spiritual sacrifice—the regenerate must sacrifice carnal passions to the divinity. This offering must be complete, and the soul unsullied and spotless. The presiding divinity of this celestial operation seems, by assuming death, to take upon him the iniquities of the guilty, and absolve them.

It may be permitted me to show the perfect identity existing between these antique mythes and Christian symbolism. The illuminators of the middle ages represent Jesus Christ in black drapery, when wrestling against the genius of evil; and the Virgin Mary often has a black complexion on paintings of the twelfth century, which pertain to Byzantine art, although falsely attributed to the Evangelist, St. Luke[c]. Mary is the symbol of the Christian church; her black colour, like that of Athor, Ceres, and Aphrodite, indicates the degree preceding initiation, or the combat of the church against darkness.

The popular language of colours preserves to black its sinister signification. The Genesis of the Parses, the Boun-dehesch, relates, that the first man and the first woman, deceived by Ahriman, yielded to temptation; after their fall they covered themselves with black clothing[d].

[a] Plutarch; compare Creuzer, tom. i. p. 65. This *black* is probably indigo.

[b] Herodoti, lib. xi. Caussin. Polyhistor.Symbolicus, lib. v. cap. 7.

[c] Lanzi, Histoire de la Peinture en Italie, tom. ii. p. 10. La Mothe-le-Vayer, p. 238. Nigra sum, sed formosa. (I am black but comely.)—Solomon's Song.

[d] Boun-dehesch, p. 378.

Thus, black worn for mourning, is authorized by the most ancient traditions. According to Horus Apollo, the black dove, in Egypt, was the hieroglyph for the widow, who remained so till death[a]; among the Greeks, designated the pains and anguish of the soul. A raven announced to Apollo the infidelity of his lover. This bird was white. A messenger of grief, he and his species were metamorphosed to black[b]. In the incantations of Hecate, a representation of this goddess was made with wax of three colours, black, white, and red, and armed with a burning torch, a scourge, and a sword. (St. Croix, tom. i. p. 193.) These three combined colours signify the love and intellect of hell, or hatred and vengeance.

Court de Gebelin relates that, among the Athenians, black was the colour of affliction; white, that of innocence, joy, and purity. Thus the expiatory ship, that every year sailed first to Crete and then to Delos, hoisted black sails at departure, and white on its return; visible symbols of mental darkness and light, of grief and joy, which followed in its wake. Theseus, neglecting, on his return, to hoist the white signal, his father, Egeus, in despair, cast himself into the sea[c]. The Greeks wore black in mourning. Pericles congratulated himself in never having caused any one to wear it (Plutarch).

The Arabs, and blazonry, give to black a signification evidently derived from traditions of initiation. It designates, amongst the Moors, grief, despair, obscurity, and *constancy*[d]. Black, in blazon, named sable, signifies prudence, wisdom, and constancy in adversity and woe[e].

On an Egyptian painting, red men are beheading black men; the former looking eastward, to the source of light, the latter westwards, to the regions of darkness. This induces a curious interpretation of Etruscan vases. With few exceptions, only two colours are visible, red and black, white serving to heighten the ornaments, though some vases are otherwise coloured. These two colours seem to present the dualism of good and evil; the red figures on a black ground relating to beneficent deities. The rites of initiation to the mysteries of Bacchus are, in fact, so represented. By opposition, black figures on a red ground indicate the idea of darkness and death.

On a vase described by Passeri, the Dioscóri are drawn on a golden yellow ground. This deviation requires notice. Yellow was the symbol of light and of

[a] Hori Apollinis Hieroglyphica, lib. ii. sect. 20.

[b] Hygin. Astronom. lib. ii. p. 75. Apollodori, lib. iii. p. 296.

[c] Monde primitif, viii. 206. The pirate's flag is black, synonymous of death or victory.

[d] Gassier, Chev. Franc. p. 351.

[e] Anselme, Palais de l'Honneur, p. 12.

the sun; the myth of the Dioscori represented the sun declining and resuscitating every six months. Castor and Pollux are of a black colour. Pollux rides a red horse, and Castor a black one. Only Pollux was immortal. He divided with his brother this heavenly gift, and condemned himself to death to give him life. The Dioscori are alternately born to die again. Does not this red horse represent life, and the black one death?

On another vase Achilles is expiring; above is Mercury, preparing to weigh the soul of the hero in a balance. A dead cow, an expiatory libation, and other symbols of death, accord with the black colour of the figures, which are heightened by a red ground [a].

Camillus, the Etrurian Mercury, was guardian of the sepulchres and conductor of the manes. He is represented of a red colour on an antique vase [b]. His wings, tunic, and buskins, are black; at his feet a black serpent rears itself, symbol of the transmigration of souls. The black colour of the vesture of the young Camillus recalls the black ring of Mercury, which opens the gates of hell. This allegory connects this urn with funereal rites. According to Passeri, it was filled with ashes.

Finally, these conjectures acquire a high degree of certainty by a comparison of Etruscan embalming with Egyptian; plates of which are in Passeri, and the Description of Egypt.

The opposition of black and red is still preserved in games of cards. Court de Gebelin states, that the game of cheques is derived from the Egyptians, and our cards are an imitation of chequers [c].

It is a curious fact that, previous to a battle, soldiers throw away playing cards as evil symbols. During the last continental war, battle fields were often strewed with them. Where true faith animates not, superstition prevails.

[a] Passeri, Pict. Etrusc., tom. iii. pl. 262, 263.
[b] Ibid. tom. iii. p. 75. pl. 297.
[c] Vide Sir Gardner Wilkinson's Ancient Egyptians.

END OF THE SECOND SECTION.

SYMBOLIC COLOURS,

IN ANTIQUITY—THE MIDDLE AGES—AND MODERN TIMES.

FROM THE FRENCH OF FRÉDÉRIC PORTAL.

WITH NOTES.

By W. S. INMAN, Assoc. Inst. Civil Engineers.

THIRD SECTION.

OF GREEN.

DIVINE LANGUAGE.

In commencing this section, it may be necessary to recapitulate the principles we have adopted. In the symbolic generation of colours there are three degrees : 1st, Self existence; 2nd. Manifestation of life; 3rd. Action resulting therefrom. In the first, love or the will presides, indicated by red; in the second intellect appears, designated by blue; finally, in the third, action exhibits its symbol in green. According to the prophets, three spheres emanate from God, which occupy the three heavens; the first, or sphere of love, is red; the second, or sphere of wisdom, is blue; the third, or sphere of creation, is green. In the Bible the Eternal is represented dwelling on an azure throne, surrounded by a flaming sphere[a]. In the Apocalypse he appears in the centre of an emerald rainbow[b]. These spheres, named limbi, were imitated on Indian paintings, and also in those of the Middle Ages.

[a] Ezekiel, chap. i. verse 26. Exod. chap. xxiv. verses 9, 10.
[b] Apocalypse, chap. iv. verse 3.

PART VI.—ARCH. II.   B

Three degrees of regeneration correspond to the three celestial spheres; they are again found in antique initiation, with their three symbolic colours, red, blue, and green, indicating fire, air, and earth. Mythology presents numerous proofs of the universality of the dogma of the celestial spheres: the philosophy of the Hindhus (Colebrooke, p. 169,) reproduces it in explaining the mystic syllable *Om*, composed of three elements of articulation.

Hindhus, Persians, Scandinavians, and all aboriginal nations represent the Divinity in a human form[a]. A drawing of Brahma-Sami in Langlè's " Monumens de l' Hindoustan" explains these symbolisms. Vischnou, or the Universal Man, has on his face the effigy of Siva, on the breast that of Krichna, on the stomach that of Brahma, and lower, that of Ganesa. The head represents the celestial kingdom where reigns God, the creator and destroyer Siva, represented by red colour as the God of Fire, *i. e.* of love divine; on the breast symbol of respiration (spiritus) appears Krichna, whose colour is blue, for he is truth divine, incarnate on earth; on the stomach, representing the intermediary world where the good and the wicked set forth, reigns Brahma, spiritual creator or regenerator of humanity by love and wisdom; red and blue are assigned to him; finally, Ganesa has the third sphere, that of Brahma being but a passage where souls undergo their last purification.

Ganesa is the god of wisdom and of marriage; green is consecrated to Ganesa[b], also to Janus, to the Egyptian Jannes, to St. John the Evangelist, and to all the divinities of paganism which represent the good and the true in the actions of life.

The two arms of the god-man, in the same drawing, indicate the creative power by wisdom and love; parallelizing the three degrees existing in the human understanding—the will, the reason, and action. The will is figured on the right shoulder by a man, and on the left shoulder by a woman. Between the arms are seen lance heads, emblems of the power of the reason, which is the spiritual arm of the will. Finally, the lotus flower inscribed on the wrists, designates divine action or the creation of the world, which is the last degree[c].

Vischnou, in the first divine sphere, is the creator by fire or by love, and is repre-

---

[a] Desatír, p. 99. The world is a man and man is a world. The giant Hymer represents this dogma in Icelandic cosmogony. Est terra creata ex Ymeris carne, mare ex ejus sanguine, saxa ex ossibus, vegetabilia ex capillis, cœlum ex cranio, &c. Finus magnusem Mythologiæ lexicon, p. 598. Comp. the Edda by Mallet.

[b] M. Portal possesses a small figure of Ganesa in green granite, and considers the coloured stones to be assigned to the divinities of paganism according to the symbolism of colours. His miniatures of the middle ages confirm it in those periods.

[c] The world was born in the calyx of a lotus.

sented red, according to a former quotation from the Bagavadam[a]. Vischnou appeared at first with a body invested with purple, more brilliant than the sun and like unto fire: such is the primitive manifestation, or in the first sphere. In the second, Vischnou reveals himself in his eternal wisdom and incarnates himself in Krichna, whose colour is blue. Finally, in the third sphere, that of the actions and customs of life, Vischnou-Krichna is painted green. On a monument in the Borgian Museum at Velletri, he appears of this colour amidst groves and meadows; not far off is a marsh, wherein swim the fishes and crocodiles which he has conquered[b]: exterior regeneration was indicated by water, fish, and green colour. This first degree was also represented by the ape Hanouman, of a green colour, which transported Vischnou-Rama on his shoulders when crossing the sea. Finally, in his incarnation into a tortoise, Vischnou has a green complexion[c]. The tortoise is the symbol of stability in the creation of the universe and the regeneration of mankind : in India and Japan the world is represented placed on a tortoise[d]. This symbol reappears in Greece in the Venus of Phidias; to Venus green was attributed, symbol of regeneration. Finally, on the obelisk of Luxor, now at Paris, Amon, the spiritual sun, the Word divine, is qualified as God, Lord of the three zones of the universe[e].

Denis the areopagite, converted to Christianity by St. Paul the Apostle, in his Treatise of the Celestial Hierarchies, states that the Angelic Intelligences are divided into three orders, in essence, in virtue, and in action. There are three heavens, each likewise divided into three. According to the Theosophy of the Armenian geographer, Vartan, there are three heavens; the spheres of fire, air, and water correspond to them in the material world.

The twelve celestial worlds of Grecian philosophy present the same dogma: according to Aristotle, the highest is the abode of the Supreme; according to Plato it is the region of Ideas; below roll the seven planets, and successively the sphere of fire, air, water, and earth appear[f]. This tenet reappears in the curious work of Rabanus Maurus on the Cross[h], and on some monuments of the middle ages. The saints represented on paintings have aureols of different colours, so have angels, but God and

[a] Bagavadam, p. 11.
[b] Paulin, Musæi Borgiani Codice, pp. 225, 226.
[c] Ibid.
[d] Kœmpfer Histoire du Japan, &c.
[e] Champollion-Figeac, l' Obelisque de Louqsor, p. 6.
[f] St. Martin, Mémoires sur l'Arménie, tom. ii. p. 407.
[g] Photii Bibliotheca, p. 1315. Edit. Rothomag.
[h] Rabani Mauri de Laudibus sanctæ crucis, MSS. de la Bibliothèque Royale, coté No. 59.

Jesus Christ alone appear in the centre of the spheres or limbi which entirely surround them; sometimes a second sphere appears below the first around the footstool of the Divinity. In the Latin Bible of the tenth century[a], Jesus Christ is surrounded by a red limbus bordered by a blue band, his aureolus is red; cherubim and angels encircle him; their aureoli are some red, some blue, and others green. Below the Saviour's feet is a purple sphere, and the footstool of the Divinity has three bands, red, blue, and green.

On a miniature of the eleventh century[b], representing the Pentecost, the Holy Ghost is in the centre of a triple sphere, blue, red, and green, whence red rays dart on the Apostles. Finally, these three celestial spheres appear twice in the Latin MS. of Biblical Emblems of the Thirteenth Century[c].

GREEN—CONSECRATED LANGUAGE.

Previous to initiation in the ancient mysteries of pagan religion and philosophy, the neophyte underwent four proofs of purification by water, earth, air, and fire, indicated by the colours green, black, azure, and red. The earth represented the chaos and darkness of the profane; water or baptism was the emblem of exterior regeneration, by triumphing over temptations; air designated divine truth, enlightening the understanding of the probationer, as fire, or the supreme degree, opened the heart to love divine. These symbolic proofs were purely exterior; they figured the four material spheres through which the neophyte must pass before attaining the three heavens represented on earth by the three degrees of initiation, or by spiritual regeneration. The first degree, granted after accomplishing the proofs, is acquired by the water of baptism and the reformation of manners; the mystic was then regenerate in his actions and exterior life; he had passed the gate of spiritual death, marked by darkness and black colour. The symbols of this first degree were the colours black and green; the black referred to the primitive waters and chaos, as the green recalled the creation: black was consecrated to marine deities, and they were invested in green costume.

The earth had likewise the same colours for symbols, as dark matter, black was attributed to it, and, as the principle of vegetation, green[d]. The motive for assigning these two colours to earth and water exists in the law of nature; vegetation is pro-

---

[a] MSS. de la Bibliothèque Royale, No. 6, tom. i.
[b] Ibid. No. 819.
[c] Emblemata Biblica, MSS. de la Bibliothèque Royale, No. 37.
[d] Green colour is consecrated to the earth by John the Lydian.

duced by the action of these two elements, green indicating their productive union, and black their state of separation and death.

Baptism was the symbol of the mystery of the creation; the profane represented inert and obscure matter; water poured over the head figured the fruitful principle which would regenerate him[a].

Thus the parable of the sower taught Christians that regeneration resembles the germ of a plant which is born again, from amidst death, and reverdant in a new life. In the Apocalypse the locusts are ordered to injure no more any verdure or tree, or herb of the earth, nor any man but those who would not have the seal of God in their foreheads[b].

The second degree of initiation, figured by blue colour, indicated spiritual regeneration. The neophyte received the baptism of the spirit, marked on Egyptian anaglyphes, by blue water.

Finally, the third degree was the baptism by fire. In the paintings on the temples of Thebes, the manes which enter into eternal life receive on their heads baptismal waters, red and blue[c]. This triple baptism appears again in the Gospel. St. John the Baptist says, (Matth. 3rd and 11th,) " I, indeed, baptize you with water unto repentance: but he that cometh after me is mightier than I, whose shoes I am not worthy to bear: he shall baptize you with the Holy Ghost, and with fire."

India affords the most ancient traditions on the symbolism of green colour: regeneration was represented under the emblem of warfare between the Supreme God Vischnou and the chief of the evil genii; in the war of Lauca, incarnate as Rama, he subdued them. These giants in India were spirits of darkness, as in Greece, Genesis, and Scandinavia; their colours give the key to this myth. In temples dedicated to this incarnation[d], Vischnou is represented coloured green, as a perfectly beautiful young man, holding a bow and arrows. Hanouman, by his side, awaits his orders; there is also a picture of a giant having ten heads of a blue colour, and twenty arms, holding in each hand different arms, emblems of strength and power. According to Sir William Jones, Hanouman, the general of the army of apes, represents the wild men of the mountains civilized by Rama; here, doubtless, the profane regenerated, for orientalists agree that in India the ape is the symbol of the soul[e]. Rama cannot subdue the giants but by crossing the sea; the apes, by prodigious labour, form a bank.

[a] Vide ancient Egyptian paintings still extant; mode of consecrating a youth.
[b] Apocalypse, chap. ix. verse 4.
[c] Description de l'Egypte, planches.
[d] Sonnerat, tom. i. pp. 289, 292. Compare Paulin. Systema Brahmanicum, p. 134.
[e] Langlès, Monumens de l'Hindoustan, tom. ii. p. 49, and numerous authorities which he quotes.

Rama, represented green, is the symbol of the first degree of regeneration ; the sea designates baptismal ablution [a], the work of the soul cannot be accomplished but by the severe labour of regeneration. The giants, personified in their chief, are distinguished by blue colour ; this symbol of divine wisdom, appropriated by an evil spirit, indicates that false human wisdom which struggles against the influence of God the regenerator : thus, the arms of the giant cannot prevail whilst those of Vischnou never fail in their object.

Rama, is identical with Bacchus, the conductor of souls, and the chief of the giants with Pluto [b].

In the first degree of regeneration, Rama is of green colour ; in the second, he is painted blue, and surnamed Blue-body, the denomination of Vischnou and Krichna, representing divine wisdom ; in the third, his body is hyacinth colour, the eyes and lips of a blood red colour—he is then the master of the world, the moiety of Vischnou himself [c]. In Egypt, the supreme degree of initiation acquired in entering another life, was represented by red and blue baptismal waters, the hyacinth colour of Rama is formed by their union.

The religions of antiquity, like Christianity, considered the Divinity in his twofold attribute of love and wisdom. The language of colours translates this universal tenet by red and blue. The mysteries reproduced this duality of the good and the true ; Venus and Minerva were the symbols of this doctrine revealed in the first degree of initiation ; their history and green colour prove it. The Egyptian Minerva, Neith, was born of the water. She was daughter of the Nile, as Minerva was the daughter of Neptune and the nymph Tritonis, or the lake Triton [d]. Her birth typifies the first degree in the mysteries, baptism.

Pallas-Athēnē at first appears in connexion and then in opposition to water ; she combats Poseidon or Neptune, before obtaining the dedication of the city which bears her name [e]. In cosmogony, divine wisdom combats the primitive waters, and creates the world from the chaotic deep : in the mysteries, the Neophyte combats his carnal passions, and by overcoming them acquires a new existence. Baptismal ablution was both a symbol of cosmogony and of initiation, of the creation of the universe, and of spiritual regeneration ; wisdom thence appears of twofold origin ;

[a] First ceremonial of the Knights of the Bath in English Chivalry.
[b] Paulin, p. 143. Langlès, tom. i. p. 184.
[c] Langlès, tom. i. p. 183. Paulin, p. 143.
[d] Pausanias, lib. i. cap. 14.
[e] Creuzer, liv. vi. chap. 8.—Thus on one pediment of the Parthenon was typified the commencement of the Mystery of Regeneration, and on the other, Elysium or the God's Association—its consummation.

emanated from God she was symbolized as Pallas issuing armed from the brain of Jupiter, and thus was represented of a red colour, as goddess of spiritual combats; and as born from regenerated man—her symbol was Minerva of a green colour.

The Neophyte cannot be regenerated but by the twofold baptism of the Spirit and of fire, by the union of truth and love. The Egyptian Minerva, Neith, espouses the God of fire, the Saite and Memphite Ptha, from this marriage the Sun is born, symbol of eternal Light, and of divine revelation. So is the Grecian Minerva united to celestial Vulcan, the God of pure fire, she gives birth to Apollo, the Sun.

Homer attributes to Minerva eyes of a bluish grey, or sea green colour (Γλαυκῶπις Ἀθήνη); Mythographers, radiant eyes of a triple colour [a], symbols of the degrees of initiation, and thus was her pallium of gold, of azure, and of purple. To this goddess was assigned the epithet *musica*. Music, or science taught by the Muses, comprised all human knowledge: Moses, said Philo, was initiated in all the music of the Egyptians; the Muses presided at its source [b], and Moses was saved from the waters, and by baptismal waters [c].

Minerva is the symbol of wisdom, and of truth, in the mysteries. Venus represents divine love. The Greeks distinguished two goddesses named Venus, the one celestial, the other terrestrial [d]—the one green, the other black. Athor, among the Egyptians, was the passive principle, the emblem of chaos and night, which enveloped nature before creation; the Greeks formed their dark Venus after this divinity. The second Venus, of a green colour, emanated from the first—she was born from the primitive waters, and took the surname of Venus Aphrogene, born from the foam of the sea; then united to Hermes, the initiator, she gave birth to Love [e]. The dark Venus represents the state which precedes regeneration, Venus Aphrogene issuing from the sea; Initiation, which commences by baptism, united to Hermes, the personification of the priesthood and sacred rites; she produces love divine. This goddess presides over carnal generation, the emblem of spiritual regeneration. Finally, Venus Regeneratrix, tends to identify her with the Sun, the symbol of love and truth, emanated from God. Thus, according to Hebrew Cabalists, Beauty, one of the ten divine emanations, (Sephiroth,) had for a symbol green and yellow [f]. These two approximated colours, reconduct us to the myth of Mitra-Mithras. Herodotus tells

---

[a] Albrici de deorum imag. p. 172.

[b] Creuzer, i. 492, 493.

[c] Vide Lacour, Traité sur les Hiéroglyphes.

[d] Pausanias.

[e] Creuzer, Histoire des Religions, i. p. 657.

[f] Matter, Histoire du Gnosticisme, tom. i. p. 102.

us that the Persians named the celestial Venus, Mitra [a], and Mithras is identical with the Sun.

We know from a passage in John the Lydian that green was consecrated to Aphrodite [b]. A painting at Herculaneum confirms this fact; it represents Venus with a flowing drapery of verditer colour [c]. The three graces, her companions, were symbols of the three celestial spheres, and of the three degrees of regeneration, that the soul must pass through to become regenerate. Thalia presides over vegetation, the colour of which is green; Euphrosyne, over the empire of the air, azure; and Aglaia over fire, or red [d].

To all Grecian marine deities sea-green colour was attributed,—to Neptune, the Nereids, Nymphs, and Rivers; in antique paintings [e]. John the Lydian confirms this; the colour of the sea (βενετον, venetus color, or Celadon) was consecrated to Poseidon or Neptune [f].

Freya, a divinity of the Scandinavians, is identified with the Venus Aphrodite of the Greeks [g]. Friday was also consecrated to her (Freytag). Freya is a marine deity. One of her appellatives is Syr, lover of waters. In the Zent-Avesta the dog Tuscher or Syrius presides over rain and the initiation of death. In Zend, Sur signifies the sea or waters. The Scandinavian Venus, daughter of Niord, god of the sea, was goddess of love; the first she taught the magic art. All these traditions relate to sacred mysteries. One more resemblance evinces the intimate relation between antique religions. Freya, like Isis, incessantly weeps for the departure of her husband. She seeks for him in a country where she has received the name of Vanadis, goddess of hope. Isis is the Egyptian Venus, according to Apuleius.

Christianity reproduces the doctrine taught in the mysteries. Jesus said (John chap. iii. verse 3), " Unless a man be born again, he cannot see the kingdom of God." The symbol of regeneration was the re-birth of nature in the spring time, the vegetation of plants, of trees, and the verdure of the fields. The Messiah, going to execution, consecrated this symbol, as he had already established it by the parable of the sower; bearing his cross, he said to those who followed him, (Luke, chap. xxiii. verse 31,)

[a] Herodoti, lib. i. p. 66, ed. Wesseling.

[b] Lydus de Mensibus, Guigniaut sur Creuzer, i. p. 550.

[c] Winkelman, Histoire de l'Art, ii. p. 188.

[d] Vide Beaudouin Mythologie.

[e] Histoire de l'Art, tom. ii. p. 187.

[f] De Mensibus.

[g] Freya Spumare ἀφρὸς, unde hellenum Freya voca est 'Αφροδίτη, Finno Magnusen, Mythologiæ Lexicon, Nota, p. 82.

" If they do these things in a green. tree, what shall be done in the dry ?" The green tree designates regenerated man, as the dry tree is the image of the profane, dead to spiritual life.

In China, green typifies the east, the spring, a tree, and charity[a]. In Christianity, green is the symbol of regeneration in action, i. e. of charity. The Messiah reminds man of the two commandments—the sole bases of eternal salvation—the love of God and of our neighbour. Offering up himself as a sacrifice, he gives an.example of that divine charity which becomes the hope of mankind. Christian painters of the middle ages painted the cross of a green colour, symbol of regeneration, of charity, of hope; sometimes it was bordered with a red band, as in the large windows of Chartres Cathedral. The sepulchre and instruments of the passion were often painted green.

The friend of Christ, the Christian initiator, the sacred scribe of the sealed mysteries in the Apocalypse, St. John, is almost always robed in green. Tradition consecrates this colour to the Virgin and infant Jesus, symbolizing the first degree of regeneration. The colour of the vestments of the Messiah, at different epochs of his life, form a sacred drama, whence we may hereafter understand the symbolism of colour.

Among the Arabs, green had the same signification; it became the symbol of initiation to the knowledge of the Supreme God, revealed in the Koran. The struggle of evil and good principles was represented by black and white. Mahomet saw legions of angels thus engaged, clothed in white; in the principal actions of his life, according to Mussulman traditions, he was succoured by these angels, with green turbans. White and green were, and remain, the colours of Islamism ; the principal ensigns of the Turkish empire are green or white; white satin forms the full dress of the grand vizier, and white cloth that of the mufti. "Both," says Mouradja, " as vicars, and representing the sovereign, the one for temporalities, the other for spiritual." Green satin is also the regulation dress of all pachas of three tails, as lieutenants of the monarch, in provinces confided to their administration; and the green cloth robe of ceremony of the Oulemas, as being the ministers of justice, of religion, and law, in the name and under the authority of the Sultan, who is the supreme imaun or chief pontiff of Islamism. The green turban is also exclusively reserved to all the emirs, descendants of Ali. Finally, this colour is become the distinctive mark not only of the Ottoman nation, but of all Mussulmen[b].

---

[a] Visdelou, Notice sur l'Y King a la suite du Chou-King, p. 428.

[b] Mouradja d'Ohsson, tom. iv. première partie, p. 161.

The character of Islamism, amongst oriental religions, is that of initiator of the knowledge of the One God : Ali, the initiator by conquest, wears a green robe[a], like St. John, the initiator by spiritual arms. The day consecrated to the God of Mahomet is Friday, the day of the Green Venus.

Green, like other colours, had a nefarious signification in opposition, it signified moral degradation and folly. The Theosophist of Sweden, Swedenborg, gives green eyes to fools in hell. A window in Chartres Cathedral represents the temptation of Jesus Christ, Satan with green eyes and skin. According to La Mothe Vayer, in ancient France green was the blazon of fools[b].

In symbolism, the eye signifies the understanding, intellectual light ; man can turn it towards good or towards evil. Satan and Minerva, Folly and Wisdom, were represented with green eyes.

PROFANE OR POPULAR LANGUAGE.

Popular legends, by materializing sacred traditions, preserve them. Green, the symbol of the regeneration of the soul, of the spiritual new birth, was the emblem of natural birth. For a long period, to the emerald was superstitiously attributed the miraculous virtue of hastening childbirth. That the neophyte must gain the victory over his passions was prefigured in the books of Genesis, the Zends, and the Eddas, by the serpent. That emerald powder cures the bite of venomous animals was a popular legend. Green was the symbol of sacred immortality, and of worldly hope. By inversion, the profane attributed to it despair. In scenic representations of Greece, in certain circumstances, sea-green was a sinister colour[c].

Green symbolized spiritual victory, afterwards material victory, and, finally, amongst the Greeks, defeat and flight[d]. Amongst the Moors green had the same signification ; it designated hope, joy, youth, spring, the youth of the year, which gives the hope of harvests[e] afterwards.

In heraldry, sinople (the green of blazonry) also signified love, joy, abundance. " Archbishops," says Anselme, " wear a hat of sinople, with interlaced cords of green silk. . . . . . Bishops likewise wear a hat of sinople, because they are

---

[a] Mouradja d'Ohsson, tom. iv. première partie, p. 163. " Mahommedanism has converted millions from idolatry to worship the only true God." Opusculis, p. 242.

[b] " Rather green," in English phraseology, still has this meaning.

[c] Julii Pollucis Onomasticon, lib. iv. cap. 18.

[d] Pollux, ibid.

[e] Gassier, Histoire de la Chevalerie Française, pp. 351, 352.

ordained as Christian shepherds; this colour denotes good pasturage, where wise shepherds lead their flocks to pasture, and it is the symbol of the good doctrine of these prelates." [a] Green was the symbol of good Christian doctrine, of good Mahometan, Indian, Grecian, and Egyptian doctrine: the last ring of this historic chain attaches itself and is connected with the first.

OF ROSE.

Rose colour derives its signification from red and white; red is the symbol of divine love; white, of divine wisdom; their reunion will signify the love of divine wisdom. Here an analogy with yellow is apparent, which likewise designates love and wisdom, and which, according to symbolism, emanates from red and white. The difference existing between these two colours is, that in the yellow, the two attributes of divinity are assimilated in unity, whilst in the rose they remain distinct. Gold and yellow have a superior signification to that of rose colour. Gold relates to God, and to his revelation, and rose indicates regenerated man, who receives the holy word.

The rose and its colour were symbols of the first degree of regeneration, and of initiation to the mysteries. There was a relation between rose colour and baptism, which opened the doors of the sanctuary, a relation which is again found in the Latin word rosa, which is evidently derived from rose, the dew, rain. Horapollo says, that the Egyptians represented the human sciences by water falling from Heaven [b]. Among this nation the sciences were within the temple's precincts, and revealed only to the initiated. The rose was likewise in Egypt the symbol of regeneration. The ass of Apuleius recovers the human form by eating a crown of vermilion roses presented him by the High Priest of Isis. In effect it is only by appropriating to himself the love and the wisdom of God, signified by red and white, and by their union in the rose, that the regenerated neophyte casts away his brutal passions, and becomes truly a man.

In the sacred books of India, the dew is the symbol of the divine word. "O great Souda, (Bagavadam, p. 6,) send down upon us the dew of thy divine word." Rose colour has the same signification. The camalata produces three beautiful flowers of a soft celestial red, the colour of love, according to the Hindhu books; the camalata has the virtue of procuring for the inhabitants of the heaven of India all they desire, by

[a] Palais de l'Honneur, pp. 12, 65.
[b] Hori Apollinis hieroglyph.

only wishing ª. The Bible confirms the signification of these Scriptures : Moses said, " My doctrine shall drop as the rain, my speech shall distil as the dew, as the small rain upon the tender herb, and as the showers upon the grass." ᵇ   We know that the herb and verdure represent the commencement of regeneration.   Isaiah said, " Thy dead men shall live, together with my dead body shall they arise.   Awake and sing, ye that dwell in dust : for thy dew is as the dew of herbs, and the earth shall cast out her dead." ᶜ   Isaiah here alludes to baptism ; the dead are the profane, the living the regenerated.   It would be difficult to misunderstand this in quoting a passage from another verse of the same prophet,   " Drop down ye heavens from above, and let the skies pour down righteousness : let the earth open, and let them bring forth salvation." ᵈ

The rose reproduces in the Bible the same idea as dew ; only the rose tree is the image of the regenerated, and the dew is the symbol of regeneration.

In Ecclesiasticus, Wisdom is " exalted as a rose plant in Jericho," ᵉ and again, " Hearken unto me, ye holy children, and bud forth as a rose growing by the brook of the field :" the brook, is it not the emblem of baptismal ablution, the source of wisdom ? A low philology may credit these as mere rhetorical figures ; our poetry is dead, and it cannot comprehend the vitality which animates Biblical poetry.   The history of each symbol, however, demonstrates that in the Prophets it is no mere question of tropes ; for these hieroglyphs again appear with the same signification among all ancient nations.

Claudian said that at the birth of Minerva, in the Isle of Rhodes, it rained gold ᶠ. Rhodes, or the isle of *Roses*, according to the Greek and Latin meaning of the word, indicates the mysteries of initiation.   At the birth of Minerva, i. e. at the birth of wisdom, or regeneration, it rained gold, because that the Neophyte received spiritual baptism, or the word divine ; the rain and the gold having this signification.   The rose was the symbol of wisdom and of love,—it ought to be consecrated to wisdom as well as to Minervà.

Venus, one of the personifications of the mysteries, adores Adonis ; *Adonai* is one of the names of God in the Bible ; Adonis was wounded to death by a wild boar, Venus metamorphosed his blood into the red anemony flower ; running distracted at

---

ª De Marles, Histoire de l'Inde, tom. ii. p. 182.
ᵇ Deuteronomy, chap. xxxii. verse 2.
ᶜ Isaiah, chap. xxvi. verse 19.
ᵈ Isaiah, chap. xlv. verse 8.
ᵉ Ecclesiasticus, chap. xxiv. verse 14, and xxxix. verse 13.
ᶠ Auratos Rhodiis imbres Nascente Minerva.

the dying voice of her lover, a thorn wounded her naked foot, the blood of the goddess gushed forth on the white rose, and tinted it vermilion.

In antiquity, the rose recalled symbols of the dead, because it was one of the symbols of initiation, the first degree of which was an imitation of carnal death. The ancients strewed roses on the tombs, and called this ceremony *Rosalia*. Each anniversary, in May, they offered to the manes of the deceased plates of roses, *rosales escæ*. This pious custom testified the new spiritual life educed from the depths of destruction.

Hecate, the *dea feralis* of the Romans, presided at death. She is sometimes represented with her head cinctured with a garland of five-leaved roses [a]. The No. 5, like the rose, indicated the commencement of a new state.

The symbolism of the middle ages reproduced the different significations attributed by antiquity to this colour amongst the Northern barbarians, remaining traditions refer to its Oriental origin, and which unite it at a later period to the emblems of Christianity.

A divinity of slaves, named Prono, was represented holding in one hand a dart, and in the other a buckler of rose colour, with white points; this buckler had the form of a plough-share. This divinity is unknown, possibly it was that, invoked in the ordeal or judgment by appeal to God, previous to the introduction of Christianity; might not its etymology, Prono, be from the German word *Probe*, proof? The plough-share was one of the instruments used for trials [b]. The colour of the buckler explains the meaning attached to its form.

The white points, emblems of innocence, are thirteen in number, the symbol of death, even before Christianity [c]. The rose colour represents the union of divine love and wisdom; the dart and the buckler having the natural signification of attack and defence, these symbols may be thus translated: in the combats against the dead or in trials, innocence finds its protection in the wisdom and love of God which it invokes.

The earliest traditions of Christianity evince perfect agreement with these different significations. In the seventh century, according to Bede, the tomb of Jesus Christ was painted of an intermingled colour of red and white [d]. The white rose became the

[a] Noe, Dictionnaire de la Fable.

[b] Prono Aldenburgensium Slavorum idolum columnæ impositum stans, altera manu vomerem, quo innocentia probari solebat, rosei coloris albis discriminatum punctis, altera vero hasta cum vexillo tenebat. (Schedius de Diis Germanis, p. 750.)

[c] The number 12 was a perfect and complete number; the number 13 indicated the commencement of a new course of a new life, and thence it became the emblem of death.

[d] Color ejusdem monumenti et sepulchri albo et rubicundo permixtus videtur. (Bed. Hist. Ang. lib. v. cap. 16.)

emblem of monastic wisdom, and of renunciation of the world. In the arms of religious societies a crown is placed, composed of branches of the white rose, with its
leaves, thorns, and flowers, denoting the chastity which is preserved amidst the thorns
and mortification of life [a]. A picture of the school of Correggio, (Musée Royale, No.
956,) is impressed with this antique symbol. St. Francis, of Assisa, presents to Jesus
red and white roses, produced in January, by the thorns on which they are twisted
to resist the temptations of the Spirit of darkness. They represent initiation to divine
love and wisdom; Janus presides over January,—the heavenly doorkeeper opens the
first degree of the mysteries. In the month of January the Sun recommences his
victorious career, and overcomes cold and darkness, emblems of evil and error. The
same symbolic idea appears in the Sunday *Lætare*, which is called *Rose Sunday* because the Pope blesses a golden rose, which is carried in procession through Rome, in
order, say the mystics, to represent the joy of the day, which shines like a rose amidst
the thorns of Lent.

OF PURPLE, OF HYACINTH, AND OF SCARLET.

Purple and Hyacinth are two gradations of the same colour, which may be easily
confounded, but which have two different significations. In antiquity, purple was a
red colour, graduated with blue ; according to treatises of blazonry, purple is composed of azure and gules [b]. Heraldry preserves the traditions of colours, if it do not
the meaning of their significations. Red predominates in purple ; in hyacinth, on
the contrary, blue is the principal colour : the Oriental hyacinth, properly so called,
is a sapphire orange [c].

In the symbolism of compound colours, the predominating gives the general signification, and the subordinate tint the modified meaning ; consequently, purple indicates
the love of truth, and hyacinth the truth of love.

Scarlet was a hue composed of red with a tint of yellow ; it was the symbol of
spiritual love, of the love of the divine Word.

The vestments of Aaron and the Hebrew priests for the service of the sanctuary
were purple, scarlet, and hyacinth. Purple predominated in all the ornaments of
the High Priest: it tinted the rochet, the ephod, and the strings of the breastplate.
He alone was permitted to wear the hyacinth tunic.

In the indications of colour, we have remarked their opposition, which is apparent

[a] Anselme, p. 66.
[b] Compare Anselme, Palais de l'Honneur, i. and xii. and La Colombière Science héroique.
[c] Brard, Traité des pierres précieuses, pp. 72, 73.

in purple, hyacinth, and scarlet.   If the first of these hues signifies the good, the second the true, and the third to the manifestation of both, it results that purple will become the symbol of evil, hyacincth of error, and scarlet of the production of evil and falsehood.   In this meaning Jeremiah said that the vestments of false prophets are of hyacinth and purple. Ezekiel reproaches Samaria for her prostitutions and being enamoured of the Assyrians, clothed in hyacinth, because they have prostituted the truth. In the Apocalypse, St. John saw horsemen clothed in cuirasses, like fire, of hyacinth and sulphur, and the heads of the horses were like the head of a lion, and fire, smoke, and sulphur issued from their mouths : and by these three plagues was the third part of mankind killed [a].   In the Apocalypse, also, the scarlet beast has an infernal signification.

Paganism acquired these symbolic traditions. The ancients perceived in the divers tints of the hyacinth bright or gloomy emblems of different degrees of virtue and vice. Solin narrates that hyacinth azured is precious for virtuous men, and unfavourable to depraved men, and that the most beautiful species shines with a mingled brilliancy of purple and light [b]. Philostratus gives to Love wings of purple and azure [c]. In the popular language of colours, hyacinth should have the signification of constancy in spiritual combats ; blue designated fidelity, and red war or battles.

St. Epiphanius [d] compares the virtues of the hyacinth to those of the salamander. Not only, says Gregory Nazianzen, the salamander lived in and delighted in flames, but more, she extinguished fire.   The hyacinth, says Epiphanius, placed in a fierce furnace is unaffected and even extinguishes it.   The salamander and the hyacinth were symbols of enduring faith, which triumphs over the ardour of the passions and extinguishes them.   Submitted to fire the hyacinth is discoloured and becomes white [e]; we may here perceive a symbol of triumphant faith.

Solin pretends that the brilliancy of the hyacinth follows the changes of the atmosphere ; that it shines under a bright sun, and obscures under a cloudy sky ; that it resists the graver, and is only to be wrought by a diamond [f]. Notwithstanding this assertion, nearly all the works of Aulo are engraved in hyacinths. The ancients were not ignorant of engraving precious stones ; but whether so or not we shall completely misunderstand them, if we suppose that all their descriptions of minerals, plants, and

[a] Apocalypse, chap. ix. verses 17, 18.   Compare Richer, Nouvelle Jérusalem, tom. ii. p. 297.
[b] Solini Polyhistor, cap. xxxiii.
[c] Πτιρὰ δι Κυανία, καὶ φοινικά. (Philost. Icon. i. p. 738.
[d] Lib. xii. de Gemmis.
[e] Brard, Traité des pierres précieuses, p. 73.
[f] Solinus, cap. 33.

animals, always related to their natural history. Symbolism formed a very important portion of them; and in what Solin says of the hyacinth, an author of the seventeenth century[a] sees an emblem of a pious man, whose soul opens to the rays of divine love, and saddens when they embrace him no more.

OF VIOLET.

When two colours are equally blended, as red and blue in the violet, the signification is derived from both primitives: thus violet will designate the truth of love and
the love of truth; it will likewise comprise the sense of purple and of hyacinth, the
union of goodness and truth, of love and of wisdom. On symbolic mediæval monuments
Jesus Christ wears a violet robe during the passion, this colour representing the complete identification of the Father and the Son.

In God love and wisdom form one alone, and the same attribute is imparted to
man. Jesus, as a type of humanity, wears a red robe and a blue mantle; casting off
his human nature to reunite himself to the Deity, he is reinvested with a violet robe;
after his glorification he is God himself, and appeared in red and white, symbols of
Jehovah. To confirm this identity of divinity in the Father and the Son, artists
sometimes give a violet robe to God, as in the windows of the Church of St. John at
Troyes. The drapery of the Virgin Mary is often of this colour, to indicate the
mother of God sacrificed to save mankind. Several MSS. anterior to the renaissance;
of the Gospels, Psalteries, and Breviaries, are written in letters of gold on purple
vellum; there are many in the Bibliothèque Royale, wherein Revelation is figured
by gold, and the passion of our Lord by violet colour.

The Holy Ghost never has violet for a symbol, but only red and blue. Violet
was typical of the mystic nuptials of our Lord and his church; the Saviour by the
divine sacrifice was the type of that which man should accomplish on earth; it is
only in this world that man can attain celestial union, for there is no marriage in
heaven. Violet was assigned to martyrs[b], because that they underwent, in imitation
of their divine Master, the punishment of the cross.

This colour was adopted as mourning by personages of exalted rank, flattery de-
creeing them the martyrs' palm. Kings and cardinals wore violet as mourning[c]:

---

[a] Caussin, Polyhistor Symbolicus, lib. xi. cap. 38.   Compare lib. ix. cap. 60.

[b] Court de Gebelin, Monde primitif, tom. viii. p. 201.

[c] Color enim violaceus lugubris nota est, præsertim apud reges quibus cardinales æquiparantur.   Ciampini Vetera Monumenta, tom. i. p. 120.

On mediæval illuminations it is sometimes seen as a pall[a]. In China also it is mourning[b]; there blue represents the dead, and red the living[c]. Red indicates vital heat, blue immortality; violet should be the symbol of resurrection to eternity. In Egyptian tombs amulets are found of this colour. The mantle of Apollo was blue or violet[d]; exiled from Olympus and incarnate on earth, this divinity kept the flocks of Admetus and Laomedon. Apollo personified the sun, and the Saviour is called the New Sun.

OF ORANGE.

Orange or saffron, composed of yellow and red, had in the highest antiquity the signification of the revelation of divine love. The Messiah is named the East, and the Grecian Aurora has a saffron coloured veil; the Muses also had saffron vestures[e]. Aurora's veil was a poetic image, the Muses' vesture recalls a sacred tradition. Saffron colour indicates the union of the love of God (red) and of the Holy Word (or), comprising all science, all the Muses. Bacchus is the representative mythe of the Holy Spirit; according to Pollux, he wore a saffron vesture, and is thus represented in scenic costume[f].

The Oriflamme was the banner of St. Denis, identical with the Grecian Bacchus[g] or Dionysios in sanctifying the soul. Its colour was purple azured and gold, the two colours producing orange were separated in the Oriflamme, but reunited in its name.

In Christianity, saffron and orange colours were symbols of God, filling the heart and illuminating the spirit of the faithful. The statutes of the order St. Esprit, created by Henry III., ordain that the knights wear a cross of yellow orange velvet on their mantles and azure ribbon round the neck[h].

In chivalry, colours were not adopted by chance. In the order of Notre Dame du Chardon, instituted by Louis II. Duke of Bourbon, in 1370, the cross, enamelled in green, bore the device " *Esperance* ;" the grand cap and collar of the knights were green[i]. The cross of " Charité-Chrétienne, created by Henry III., was *blue*, bear-

[a] Breviarum Sarisb. MSS. Bibliothèque Roy. 15me Siècle.

[b] Prévost, Histoire des Voyages, tom. vi. p. 152.

[c] Préface du Chou-King, p. xxii.

[d] Winkelman, Histoire de l' Art, tom. ii. p. 187.

[e] Creuzer, liv. vi. p. 755.

[f] Julii Pollucis Onomast. lib. iv. cap. 18.

[g] Vide of Red.

[h] Anselme, Palais de l' Honneur, p. 128.

[i] Idem, p. 129.

ing for its device, " Pour avoir *fidèlement* servi."[a] The cordon of the St. Esprit is blue ; and among all nations of high antiquity azure was consecrated to the Holy Ghost.

In divine language, saffron colour designated love divine revealed to the human soul, the union of man to God.

In consecrated language, the blended hue of red and yellow was the symbol of indissoluble marriage. The wife of the flamen dialis, or priest of Jupiter, wore a veil of this hue, and her divorce was prohibited[b] ; according to Festus it was for this reason[c] that the betrothed wore the *flammeum*, or veil of flame colour, as a felicitous omen. Virgil gives to Helen a saffron nuptial veil[d]. The *flammeum* was an emblem of the perpetuity of terrestrial marriage, as the oriflamme was of the eternity of celestial nuptials.

According to the rule of oppositions, saffron and orange designated adultery ; the marigold, by its hue, is to this day the attribute of betrayed husbands. In heraldic language, it becomes likewise the emblem of dissimulation and hypocrisy[e], and the love of falsehood. In antiquity, also, these colours represented adultery avenged ; the red signified vengeance, yellow adultery. A legend preserved by Plutarch confirms this : Callirhoe, daughter of Phocus, is sought by thirty young Beotians ; irritated by refusal, they kill the father and pursue the daughter : war ensues, the pretenders are stoned, and from the tomb of the avenged victim saffron flows[f].

The ancients strewed on tombs saffron coloured flowers, perhaps to appease the avenging divinities[g].

OF TAN.

The philosopher Phavorinus said, that the eye perceives greater variety of colours than words can express[h]. If every gradation of colour represented a demonstrable idea, and we could distinguish their diversity, its language would be the most extensive and facile medium for transmitting thought. Its symbolism is not so elaborate, for language can assign names to but very few combinations of colour. Aulus Gel-

---

[a] Anselme, Palais de l' Honneur, p. 137.

[b] Auli Gellii Noctes Atticæ, lib. x. cap. 15.

[c] Festus verbo flameo.

[d] Et pictum croceo velamen acantho. Eneid, lib. i. p. 715. Compare verse 653.

[e] La Colombière, Science Héroique, p. 224.

[f] Compare Creuzer, Religions de l' Antiquité, liv. vi. p. 755.

[g] St. Croix, Mysteres du Paganism, tom. i. p. 286.

[h] Auli Gellii Noctes Atticæ, lib. ii. cap. 26.

lius has proved the poverty of Greek and Latin for the phraseology of colour[a]. His observations relate chiefly to red (Rufus color), by which the Romans designated the hue of red and black, as well as of red and yellow, and other compounds of red. Translators have further obscured the definition of these tints. It is often difficult to recognise the hue designated in their monumental inscriptions, so likewise in paintings of antiquity and the middle ages, which have suffered by time. The colour of glass and enamel changes by the action of fire, by the quality of minerals employed in them, and by the manipulation and drying of the tints.

Fire, in all ancient religions, was the symbol of divine love: the history of sacrifices evinces it; everywhere victims consumed on the pile of wood formed the basis of worship, as love is the basis of all religion.

Self-love, egotism, the principle of all crime and vices, that devouring intenseness of hatred and the passions, should have the same symbol—fire. In Leviticus, this word is used in its twofold signification. Nadab and Abihu, sons of Aaron, took censers and incense, and presented themselves before the Eternal with fire obtained from a prohibited place; immediately they went forth from his presence, fire consumed them[b]. The Bible, like the sacred books of ancient nations, is written in symbolic language: the critic Voltaire should have remembered this. For Christians St. Paul's testimony is unexceptionable; he teaches us that the passage of the Red Sea, the manna in the desert, the water gushing from the rock, were typical[c]; the Fathers of the Church have so explained them.

The infernal fire, in opposition to the divine, had smoke and ashes for particular symbols; smoke, which obscures flame, was the emblem of the darkness of impiety; ashes indicated spiritual death, the consequence of egotism, which devours and destroys its celestial heritage. Amongst the Hebrews, to cover with ashes was the sign of mourning and of the most profound grief; fire and smoke in the Prophets and Apocalypse represented the evils and falsehood of hell.

Hosea says, that the wicked have made their heart like an oven; "they shall be as smoke out of the chimney."

"Impiety," says Isaiah[d], "burneth as the fire; it shall devour the briars and thorns, and shall kindle in the thickets of the forests, and they shall mount up like the lifting up of smoke. . . . . The people shall be as the fuel of the fire:

---

[a] Auli Gellii Noctes Atticæ, lib. ii. cap. 26.
[b] 6 Levit. chap. xi. verse 3.
[c] Corinth. chap. x. 1st Ep.
[d] Isaiah, chap. ix. verses 18, 19.

no man shall spare his brother." Thus wickedness finds its *symbol* in the devouring earthly fire, and arrogance in the smoke which is inseparable from it.

Fire, smoke, and sulphur, which issue from the mouths of the horses in the Apocalypse, correspond to the images of depraved love and perverted intellect [a].

The Bible makes such frequent use of these emblems, that to refer to each would be to cite the greater part of the prophetical Scriptures. I will limit myself to one other passage, which explains a pagan legend. Abraham "looked towards Sodom and Gomorrah, and toward all the land of the plain, and beheld, and lo, the smoke of the country went up as the smoke of a furnace." Thus the crimes personified by these two cities were material, in the literal sense, or spiritual and religious, in the spirit and genius of the Holy Bible; it is equally certain that reprehensible love is represented in the sacred language by fire and smoke.

In the land of Sodom, says Solin, grow fruits, beautiful to the eye, but void of nourishment to man; their rind is covered with a sooty substance as from small cinders, which if touched exhales and falls into ashes [b].

The colour of the burning coal—the red-black, a mixture of fire and smoke, ashes and soot—is the symbol of infernal love and of treason, as proved from the book of Genesis, and in Christian symbolism.

Esau, Isaac's first-born, was red, and for this reason was named Edom, that is to say, fire-coloured, according to the version of the seventy. The word Edom is used in Genesis, in that part where Esau says to Jacob, "Give me, I pray thee, to eat of this Edom," which is there translated "red pottage;" the colour of Esau and the food for which he sold his birthright were doubtless symbolic. Esau was betrayed by his brother.

In the Apocalypse, St. John [c] sees Satan under the form of a red dragon; and there appeared, he adds, another wonder in heaven—a great red dragon, and this great dragon was the old serpent called the Devil and Satan.

The four horses in the Apocalypse, distinguished by four colours, are easily interpreted.

The first horse was white, and he that sat on him had a bow, and a crown was given unto him, and he went forth conquering and to conquer.

The second horse was red, and power was given to him that sat thereon to take away peace from the earth, and that they should kill one another; and there was given unto him a great sword.

[a] Apocalypse, chap. ix. verses 17, 18.
[b] Solin, chap. 36.
[c] Apocalypse, chap. xii. verses 3, 4.

The third horse was black, and he that sat on him had a balance in his hand.

The fourth horse was pale, and his name that sat on him was Death, and Hell followed with him [a].

The white horse indicates the power of light over darkness, good over evil, and truth over falsehood. The red horse is the symbol of quenched love, or good destroyed: when love divine no longer animates mankind, war arises and the people are slaughtered.

The black horse represents falsehood; as the red horse is symbolical of evil. The ancients distinguished two sorts of black, one which was the negation of red; that is, the tawny of red fire colour of the Apocalypse; and the second the black, the negation of white. He who sat on the black horse held *a pair of balances* which denote the estimation of the good and the true represented by the wheat and barley the quantity of which is so trifling as to be valueless.

The pale horse bears death—that spiritual death which entered the world when love and wisdom were banished from it.

Pagan traditions attach the same significations to the tawny colour, the emblem of fire and hell.

The genesis of the Parsees asserts that Ahriman moves on the fire; he sends forth from it the smoke—an obscure smoke—mingled with a great number of vapours. He unites himself to the planets,—measures himself with the starry heavens—mingles himself with the fixed stars, and all that has been created; and immediately the smoke ascends from the various places where he has made fire [b].

The Hebrew Cabalists, who had partly borrowed their dogmas from the Persians, asserted that "*severity*," one of the ten divine emanations (Sephiroth) was characterized by a red and black fire [c].

In India, the same symbols represent the same ideas : the divine love which rests in the heart, is, according to the philosophy of the Hindhu, a clear smokeless flame ; we must consequently infer that the fire obscured by smoke is the symbol of the love of evil [d].

Seeva is the principal destroyer and regenerator in the Indian mythology ; he was born in tears. Every evil which afflicts humanity comes from Seeva; he is represented covered with ashes, his hair emitting flames ; he wears a collar of human sculls ; his colour is brown [e].

[a] Apocalypse, chap. vi. verse 2.

[b] Boun Dehesch, p. 355.

[c] Matter, Histoire du Gnosticisme.

[d] Colebrooke, Philosophy of the Hindoos, p. 171.

[e] Extrait du Shaster, discourse preliminaire du Bhaguat-geeta, p. 115. Compare Creuzer, Religions de l'Antiquité, tom. i. p. 160.

Seeva is the representation of material death and spiritual regeneration: under the first aspect he is of a brown colour, and in the second, where the symbol of light triumphant over darkness is attributed to him, he is represented " *white*."

He who invoketh in the sacrifice named Asseea-Medea[a], shall fill a human skull with water wherewith he shall bedew every one who shall assist at the sacrifice: then he shall appear as the god Seeva, of a white colour, dressed in the skin of a tiger, his body covered with ashes girded with serpents; after which he shall again present himself to the god, after which he shall offer the sacrifice to him, and shall say: "Seeva, you are a demon; you are the chief of demons! You remove from us every thing which can hurt us; disperse hence every demon that they may not disturb my sacrifices. Since it is only you who have the power to put them to flight, to you I address myself—deign to grant my prayer."

The Indian paintings confirm the import of the colour brown: a monument in the Borgian Museum at Veletri[b], represents two giants covered with sacred vestments; they are communing how to deliver to death the god Chrishna; the face of the one is red, the other green; the character of these two personages is expressed on their countenances by the representative colours of infernal egotism and infernal folly in the last degree. These colours take hence their signification negative or contrary; but lest the meaning of these symbols should be misunderstood, the same subject is reproduced in positive colours. The two giants are nude, one is dark red or tawny, the other is completely black; here may still be traced infernal egotism and infernal falsities absolute.

On the first subject, the two giants are clothed in sacred vestments, and they borrow the sacred colours which they falsify. In the second subject, they are nude and appear in their real nature: they not only deny the good and the true, but they affirm the evil and the false.

The creeds of Egypt are more in accordance with those of the Hebrews than the doctrines of India or Persia; the tan colour would have the same signification at Thebes as in India. Terrible and odious darknesses, says Pimander, were suppressed, and it seemed to me that they were changed into the humid principle; agitated, they exhaled smoke like a fire[c]. Such is the principle—here is the application.

According to Plutarch and Diodorus of Sicily, the Egyptians represented Typhon of a red colour, a mixture of red and black, or, to use a Greek expression, of the

---

[a] Asseea-Medea. Dubois, Theogonie des Brahmes, p. 42.
[b] Paulin, Musæi Borgiani Codices, MSS., p. 225.
[c] Pimander, cap. i.

colour of fire [a]. Typhon is the personification of evil; it is not alone (remarks Plutarch) the heat, or the wind, or the darkness which are represented by Typhon, but all things noxious [b]. Every thing in nature of a brown colour, viz., red-black, was consecrated to Typhon; it was for this reason that, in the dog days, the kings of Egypt sacrificed and burned the red men on the tomb of Osiris [c]. These sacrifices, mentioned by Manetho, were extinct in the time of Diodorus Siculus, who speaks of them as an ancient custom. This observation is remarkable, since it proves that the degradation of the Egyptian worship may be traced to the remotest antiquity. Human sacrifice was a moral symbol materialized: the first divine revelation had taught men that they should immolate their carnal nature by sacrificing their selfish passions; initiation was consequently a type of death.

Human sacrifice was abolished in Egypt and replaced by red-coloured oxen, doubtless derived from the primitive institution prescribed to the Hebrews in the ceremonies of the lustral waters, by which the unclean man is purified [d], after having collected the ashes of a red heifer that is burned without the camp, and the priest shall take cedar wood, and hyssop with scarlet, and cast it into the sacrificial fire [e].

The Egyptian symbolism reproduced not only the Mosaical types, but it reappeared in Christianity. Typhon, the evil genius, of a red colour, took the form of a serpent, as the red dragon, who is the Devil and Satan in the Apocalypse.

The Greek fables, were they borrowed from Egypt, India, or Persia, or were they of the Hellenic soil? Be it as it may, in the mythology of this people the same symbolic dictionary is employed, as is discoverable among other nations which preceded this in civilization; of which the colour which now occupies our attention offers another example.

Love divine and infernal love had their opposite symbols in the pure or celestial fire, and in the impure or terrestrial. The Grecian Mythology reproduces this dogma in the god of pure fire—the celestial Vulcan, husband of Minerva and father of the sun—and the terrestrial Vulcan, the enemy of the sun, the abhorred husband of Venus, and father of two monsters, Cacus and Cæculus.

Vulcan, the enemy of Apollo, identifies himself with Typhon, the enemy of Osiris, and with Cain the murderer of his brother. Cain, Tubal-cain, and Vulcan are the

---

[a] Diodori Siculi, lib. i. p. 79.

[b] Plutarch de Iside.

[c] Diodorus Siculus, lib. i. p. 79. Jablonski, Panth. Ægypt. lib. v. p. 44. Witsii Ægyptiacâ, p. 33.

[d] Numbers, chap. xix.

[e] Lenoir, Explication des Hiéroglyphes.

inventors of the art of forging in metals [a]; they represent the subterraneous or infernal fire, as Abel, Apollo, Abelios, and Osiris are the symbols of celestial fire.

Vulcan is cast from heaven on account of his repulsive ugliness; in falling upon the earth he is received into the arms of the inhabitants of Lesbos; but, here below, his deformity became still more hideous: in his fall he broke his leg, and became a cripple. This divinity was the symbol of those shameful and evil passions which were expelled from heaven, and deform the world.

The dark fire of the forges and the iron are the two symbols of the evil and the false, which we shall meet with in all the sacred codes.

The black Cyclops, children of Neptune and Amphytrite, are the servants of Vulcan; inhabitants of the dark caverns, their destiny is toil. The character of the profane may be traced in this fable. The Cyclops, who have but one eye to guide them in their dark retreats, are dead to spiritual existence; they can only acquire life by becoming the children of Neptune and Amphytrite, that is to say, by initiation in water.

Beside the Cyclops appear the children of Vulcan, Cacus and Cæculus, hardened sinners who will never attain life at the baptismal sources; they are blind as the turbulent mob, who are besotted in the darkness of ignorance and vice. The ferocious Cacus emits torrents of black fire [b].

Greek fable pursues these allegories derived from Egypt. Typhon espouses Neph, the Egyptian Venus; Osiris unites himself to this goddess, but secretly; in like manner Vulcan marries Venus, and Mars seduces her. Mars was the symbol of divine love, which wrestles in the heart of man to regenerate it. Venus represents moral beauty acquired by initiation; Vulcan was the personification of evil, the embodiment of the carnal passions of man. The myth sung by Homer [c] was doubtless a sacred legend, of which it is easy to trace the sense.

The marriage of Vulcan and Venus represents the union of the soul and body. Mars, or divine love exalts the soul above earthly affections, but the human mind, typified by the material sun, averts the passions which it developes, and, under the symbol of Vulcan, entangles Mars and Vulcan in imperceptible but indissoluble ties. This first part of the fable testifies that man can do no good thing of himself, and that his intelligence only serves to rivet his earthly chains. The second part of the poem of Demodocus relates to the initiation which delivers the soul from its carnal bondage.

[a] See Genesis, chap. iv. verses 19–30.
[b] " Huic monstro Vulcanus erat pater : illius atros
      Ore vomens ignes, magnâ se mole ferebat."—Virgil Æneid, lib. 1.
[c] Odyssey, viii. 266.

The Gods hasten to accomplish the vengeance of Vulcan; Apollo demands of Hermes if he may pass the night in the arms of the fair Venus, and Hermes-Annubis is the conductor of the initiations; his costume is chequered white and black, to indicate that he conducts to light the souls plunged in darkness; but Hermes is only the mes-'senger of the Gods, he cannot of himself break the chains of Vulcan;—this honour belongs to Neptune, the god of Waters. Vulcan yields to his demand, and restores liberty to the fettered pair. The first degree of initiation, was it not by baptismal ablution? Harmony was produced by the union of Mars and Venus[a]; this divinity was the personification of sacred music, that is to say, of the knowledge required in initiation, and which restored harmony between the Creator and the creature. Minerva Musica and Moses, instructed in all the learning of the Egyptians, have illustrated this fact.

Again, the sacred mysteries of Greece narrate that Cadmus, after having brought into Greece the alphabet, and the worship of the Egyptian and Phœnician divinities, espoused Harmony, who had taught the Greeks the first elements of the art which bears his name. The connexion of all these narratives evidently demonstrates one sole idea which the Priests interpreted by the adventures of Osiris and Neph, of Mars and Venus. Osiris, the god of Light; Mars, the god of War, overcomes and captivates beauty. Thus, the man who is regenerate, fights against his earthly passions, triumphs over his fallen nature, and from the arms of death springs upward to his Creator—to the God of armies, the God of victory, of peace, and harmony.

The antagonism of the love of good and the love of evil, receives a new form in the mysteries of Eros and Anteros. Eros is the divinity of love; Anteros is his oppo-nent or the contrary. In profane language, Anteros was the emblem of reciprocal love; but in the esoteric doctrine of the temples, Anteros was born of Night and Erebus; his companions were inebriety, grief, and contention; his leaden arrows excite the brutal passions, which drag satiety in their train, whilst true love flings golden darts which inspire a pure joy and virtuous and sincere affection.

Eunapius relates, in the life of Porphyry, that philosophy evokes these two divinities. Eros appears white as the lotus, and with golden hair; Anteros, black and red-haired[b].

The myth of Attis informs us further, that the red black was in Greece assigned to traitors.

---

[a] Apollodore, lib. iii. sect. 2.

[b] Αἱ κόμαι μιλάιτιραί τι καὶ ἡλιῶσαι. See Eunapius de Vitis philosophorum, p. 27.

The Earth enjoins his son never to quit him; Attis flies from him; escaped to the borders of a forest, Corybas, or the Sun, engages a lion of red-black colour to accuse him [a].

The symbolism of gems offers an example from the signification of the colour fawn or tawny.

The agate, according to the poem of Orpheus on Stones, is of various colours: but the most precious species is of a lion fawn colour, interspersed with heroic spots [b], yellow, white, black, and green. This stone cures the poison of the scorpion, enables woman to humanize and sweeten the life of man.

Under its auspices, the traveller returns joyous to his home with the riches he has amassed. The sick are restored to health; those who retain this stone in their hand will never be conquered. " Reflect," adds Orpheus, " wherefore Clotho has cut the thread of life? Why has his last day come?"

The dun-coloured stone is the emblem of the carnal man given up to his passions; the three colours, white, yellow, and green, indicate the three mystical degrees, or God, revelation, and regeneration; black denotes the temptations and errors; these spots are named heroic, for life is a warfare of truth against error, and of love divine against egotism. He who possesses the celestial qualities of this stone can never be vanquished when Clotho cuts the thread of life; by death, he acquires the prize of victory—the crown of immortality.

" Beware," continues Orpheus, " arm thyself against the black race of the serpent, and know that the stone is ensanguined which thy companions are destined to drink with nymphs in the cup of the Naiads." It would be impossible to indicate the mysteries more clearly for the initiated.

The Icelandic mythology, in reproducing the same dogma, seems to translate this last passage of Orpheus. At the end of the world, according to Volaspa, brothers will rise against brothers; parents forget the ties of relationship; life will be a burthen; the earth will be full of adulterers,—barbarous age of the sword, age of the tempest, age of the ravening wolf!

The shields will be broken in pieces, and incessant woes will follow each other to the end of the world; then the black, prince of fire, will go forth from the south surrounded by flames, and the universe will be consumed in a black fire. A single pair will escape the conflagration and the universal deluge; they will be nourished

---

[a] Sainte Croix, Mystères du Paganisme, vol. i. p. 90.

[b] Demi-divines ἡμιθέοισι.

by the dews, and produce such a numerous posterity, that the earth will soon be re-peopled *.

The last couple being nourished by dew, that is to say, the love and wisdom of God, explains to us the chapter on the rose colour. The further signification of this symbol cannot be doubtful, since the new existence of regenerate man is opposed to the views of the extirpated race. The black race of the serpent and the cup of the Naiads spoken of by Orpheus, is discoverable in the black prince of the genii of fire, and the dew of the Volaspa.

Christian symbolism reproduces these different significations attached to the dun colour by antiquity. The red dragon of the Apocalypse, and the red fire of hell, mentioned by the Evangelists, indicate the mode in which we are to interpret the red black employed in the stained glass and pictures of the middle ages.

The Cathedral of Chartres here offers an example worthy the attention of archeologists: over the grand entrance door, under the rose window, to the right, a stained glass represents the Indian cosmogony, as it is described in the Bhagavadam[b]. On the window of Chartres, Vischnou, draped in blue and red, reposes on a sea of milk, of a yellowish white; above him is the red rainbow: from the bosom of Vischnou issues the white lotus. The upper window represents Brahma with his quadruple face and the crown on his head. Brahma is nearly naked, his skin is bistre or dun; he wears saltirewise a green mantle, which envelopes the lower part of his body; he reposes on the lotus, and in each hand he holds a stem. The upper windows, separated by iron bars, represent corresponding subjects. Finally, on the last and most elevated, Jesus appears, clothed in a blue robe, and wearing a bistre coloured mantle; above his head descends the Holy Ghost, in the form of a dove. The lotus issuing from the bosom of Vischnou rises up to Jesus Christ, where it appears in full blossom.

This window, much anterior to the period of the renaissance, proves the communication of the Oriental myths at the epoch of the crusades; it unites the symbols of Christian with those of Indian initiation.

Satan is sometimes exhibited with four faces on paintings of the middle ages. I have seen two examples in biblical emblems in a MS. of the 13th century, in the Bibliothèque Royale; the windows of Chartres will be nearly as old[c]. Thus the design and colour of Brahma connect him with infernal genii,

---

[a] Edda, Fables, 32, 33, and remarks of Mallet.
[b] Bhagavadam, p. 62.
[c] Emblemata Biblica, MSS. de la Bibliothèque Royale, coté No. 37.

In the Cathedral of Chartres the red brown or bistre is frequently used to pourtray the above mentioned symbolisms. On the first ogee of the side nave of the choir, to the right, is a representation of the Lord's Supper; on the left of Christ appear two of his disciples, disputing with each other; Jesus is beckoning them; these two persons are evidently Judas, who betrayed his Lord, and Peter, who denied him. Tradition assigns red hair to Judas.

At the foot of this picture appears the devil; his complexion is brown, with a red beard, his tunic or robe is green; at the right hand Jesus is pourtrayed, dressed in a bistre mantle, being tempted of Satan, who is here represented of a red colour, wearing a white tunic; this change of costume denotes the circumstance of the temptation. Satan borrows the language of the Most High; the colours vary according to the progress of the temptation; on the left of this representation another window depicts Jesus still wearing his bistre mantle; here the complexion of Satan is green with large green eyes, his head and robe are red.

In the upper part of this ogee appears the Virgin draped in blue; on her knees reposes the infant Jesus, dressed in bistre: this colour here denotes that Jesus was born of a woman, and subject to the sorrows of humanity, that he might procure man's salvation.

A manuscript of the eighteenth century, (one of the most curious in the Royal Museum,) proves that the red-black was symbolic of the infernal genii. Two devils of this colour seize the soul of a man who precipitates himself from the height of a tower; this picture recalls one of the figures in a game of chess, explained by Court de Gebelin [b]. On the same page, appears the descent from the cross; the cross is of a dark red, for Jesus has conquered hell by this last trial [c]. Finally, the same manuscript represents St. Michael casting into the earth a dark dragon, evidently the red dragon of the Apocalypse.

The Christian symbol, like that of the ancient, appropriates the colour of the dead leaf for the type of spiritual death. We perceive by experience, says La Colombière, that when the herbs or the leaves of trees begin to wither, they fade from their verdure into a yellow; the blue, the celestial colour, which gives them life, is evaporated, they become of a dark yellow, which for this reason we term the dead leaf [d].

[a] MSS. Coté, No. 641.
[b] Monde primitif, tom. viii. p. 176.
[c] I possess a group sculptured in wood, and painted, which represents Jesus Christ snatching souls out of hell; the devil is black and red; the souls are bistre, the body of Christ bistre, his mantle black and lined with red.
[d] Science héroique.

The water-meadows of Nimrim, saith Isaiah, shall be desolate, for the hay is withered away, the grass faileth, there is no green thing[a].

The green leaf was the symbol of regeneration, as the dead leaf that of moral degradation. The material universe appears as hieroglyphical of the spiritual world; if the doctrine cannot be borne out by facts, it is at all events neither deficient in poetry nor grandeur. The mysticism of all these epochs borrows everywhere the same language. The visions of the sister Emmerick offer an example of this assertion. She sees hell as a globe of dark fire. Caiaphas was a man of grave appearance; his countenance was fiery and menacing; he wore a long mantle of dark red, ornamented with flowers and fringes of gold[b].

The tan or brown colour was used both in ancient and the middle ages as a token of mourning. The Jews covered themselves with black or brown hair-cloth[c]. On the ancient pictures representing the passion of Jesus Christ, the personages are frequently depicted clothed in brown. Several religious orders adopt this costume as the symbols of the renunciation of the world, and of the combat which must be maintained against hell. The Moors attached the same ideas to this colour; it was with them emblematic of every evil; allied to other colours, it bears an inauspicious meaning, as will be observed by the following catalogue:

White and tan or dun	Self-sufficiency.
Red and tan	Loss of fortitude.
Green and tan	Laughter and weeping.
Black and tan	Sadness; intense grief.
Blue and tan	Patience in adversity.
Carnation and tan	Happiness and misery.
Violet and tan	Transient love.
Grey and tan	Doubtful hope; constrained patience; comfort in affliction.
Tan and white	Repentance; feigned innocence; unequal justice; dissembled joy.
Tan and red	Assumed courage; carking care; uncontrolled grief.
Tan and violet	Love disquieted; hypocrisy.
Grey, tan, and violet	Infidelity, or trust in deceitful love[d].

[a] Isaiah, chap. xv. verse 6.
[b] La douloureuse passion de notre Seigneur Jesus Christ, pp. 118–124.
[c] André Lens, Costumes de l'Antiquité, p. 223.
[d] Gassier, Histoire de la Chevalerie française, p. 352.

The tan or brown is comprised, according to the science of heraldry, of gules and sable, that is to say, of red and black; it is not used in the heraldry of France, but it was adopted by some foreign nations, and particularly by the English[*].

OF GREY.

The mixture of white and black, or grey, was, in Christianity, the emblem of terrestrial death and spiritual immortality. In Europe, mourning is first black, then grey, and lastly, white, a triple symbol of immortality.

In the religious paintings of the middle ages, grey represents the resurrection from the dead, particularly the resurrection of the body; the union of these two colours, distinctive of God and matter, easily explains the doctrine of the soul being reunited to an immortal body in a future world. These observations result from the examination of several pictures of the fourteenth and fifteenth centuries, which represent the last judgment.

One of these paintings, which I have in my possession, depicts Jesus Christ placing his feet on the sun; he is seated on a circle of gold, a hieroglyphic which, in Egypt, represents the course of the sun, and a fulfilled period; the golden circle is here likewise the sign of the close of a grand cycle or the end of the world, and is followed by the last Judgment. Our Lord is encompassed with a red halo, which, as it spreads, becomes yellow and blue; these three colours, emblematic of the Trinity, denote the omnipotence of Christ. The mantle in which he is arrayed is grey, lined with green; in general, the exterior colour of the mantle has reference to the exterior or physical man, as the interior is typical of the spiritual man or the soul. The robe of Christ is here significant of the resurrection of the body promised to the regenerated.

Two apostles kneeling are imploring the Divine mercy the while; at the sound of the angelic trumpet, two of the dead burst from their sepulchres. The angel of the judgment has green wings, which denotes the nature of his message, regeneration and new life; his red robe indicating the kingdom of heaven, which is love divine. The picture is divided into two parts representing the elect and the condemned. At the right of the Deity is St. Peter; his robe is blue, and his mantle rose; these colours indicate the baptism of the spirit [blue], and the life of love and wisdom [the rose]. Above the apostle, one of the elect, surrounded by a golden halo, rises from the tomb.

St. John the Baptist is on the left of Christ; he wears a black tunic enriched with gold; his beard and hair are green; he implores the divine clemency for those

* La Colombière, Science héroique, p. 33.

men who have received the rite of baptism, (indicated by the green beard and hair,) whilst that their souls (denoted by the black tunic) remain dead to the light of divine grace, prefigured by the golden fillet.

Beneath St. John rises one of the condemned, his black hair forming a contrast to the golden hair of the elect. This painting recalls to mind the fable of Eros and Anteros[a].

Two vignettes in the Salisbury Breviary, of the fifteenth century, now in the Royal Museum, represent the same subject with some variation. In a purple and green sphere, surrounded by yellow rays, is the Holy Trinity; the first and second persons are covered with a grey mantle, lined with green. One signification of white is *innocence;* by contrast, black expresses guilt: the reunion of these two colours, or grey, indicates in the profane language of colours, innocence calumniated, *blackened,* condemned by opinion or the laws.

Froissart relates a singular anecdote which is explained by the symbolism of colours; in 1386, the Lord of Carouges accuses James the Grey of having seduced his wife; a duel is the result, James is defeated; he dies, and his innocence is established.

Red, in the material and popular sense, indicates vengeance—blood; as *grey,* signified innocence, slander, &c.

An Icelandic legend appears to have given rise to this popular tale; Karl le Rouge, who, for abbreviation, is called Carouges, is the personification of vengeance and wars of clanship, so prevalent in the north of Europe during the middle ages; the second person, surnamed *Grey,* promises to assist Charles the red in one of his expeditions; in the mean time he cautions the enemy, and at the field of battle presents himself as the antagonist of him whom he had assured of his protection. Has Grey broken his avowed faith? Is it thus he makes proof of his boasted fidelity? The doubt here expressed is signified by his name[b].

I find another vestige of the symbolism of colours in the word GREY, taken in the sense of inebriety. Reason and wisdom were represented by white; as the debased passions by black.

SUMMARY.

One great fact governs these researches, which I submit to the learned, viz., the unity of religion among men; in proof of which, the signification of Symbolic

[a] See the Chapter on the Tan Colour.

[b] See the Times journal of the 13th September, 1835, which borrows this Icelandic Legend from the Morgenblatt.

Colours is the same in every nation and every age. Religion and the symbolism of colours follow in the same track; the one is typical of the other. The history of all religions recognises the fall of man, and the three epochs, divine, sacred, and profane, is reflected in the triple signification of colours.

It is then true that symbolism was a language revealed to man, and that man, so far from creating it or handing it down in its original purity, impressed on it the seal of human degradation.

Moreover, what does the language teach us? It teaches that the God of Moses was the God of the Pharaohs, of the Bramins, and of the Chaldees; he created man for happiness, but man forsaking the path marked out for him, fell into evil. The redemption of the world became subsequently the universal creed; Christianity, hidden or revealed, was the centre of every worship before and after God "was made manifest in the flesh."

The unavoidable conclusion is, that Christianity is the consequence and bond of all religion; that by the Divine power the whole world will be united in one common brotherhood, and in the preservation of various exterior forms the light which emanates from Divine truth may be discerned.

Mahommedanism among the nations of the East was the first degree of initiation. The unity of the Deity became the doctrine of the majority of mankind; Providence has never abandoned his work.

Already Islamism toils heavily, deriving from Christianity the life which has forsaken it. In India, Egypt, as in Constantinople, Mahommedanism gives way to European civilization. The conquest of India by the English, the expedition of the French in Egypt, and their establishment in Algiers, seem as steps marked out by Providence for attaining the great end of universal regeneration. The progress of society, the confusion in politics, and in the various modes of Christian worship, does it not forebode the dawn of a new era?

CONCLUSION.

Such are the final sentiments of the Baron Frederic Portal on Symbolic Colours, but we will not venture into the vortex of politics. The pursuits of the architectural student are of a peaceful nature: "Usui civium decori Urbium," is the legend of his Institute. This Essay opens a new prospect, extending to the remotest periods of history. Let not the tyro be deterred by unperceived analogies, or by the immortal Newton's imperfect analysis of colour. The Fine Arts are related, and based on moral and refined principles. Let us remember that pithy sentence of Plato. "The most ignorant are those who are ignorant of their own ignorance." Much ancient art is now unknown; research into its archæology will repay the labour. A coincidence in modern constructive art curiously illustrates this remark : the largest steam-vessels and men-of-war are about 250 feet long ; Noah's ark was more than double this length. A scientific periodical states that fifty years' theory, and at least half that period of practical knowledge, has elicited for the best proportions for steam-vessels the following results :—

Length of keel 1
Breadth of beam . . . . . ⅓th or
Depth of vessel 𝟷/₁₀th

The dimensions of Noah's ark were :—

			Cubits.	
Length	. . . .	300	say	= 1
Breadth	. . . .	50	.	= ⅙th
Height	. . . .	30	.	= 𝟷/₁₀th

The proportions are identical.

The people of the world, before the flood, scoffed at Noah's labour ; and when he and his family were shut up a week previous to the deluge, without any appearance of rain, ridicule was at its height, and scoffers and sneerers triumphant. The next week where were they ?

We sympathize with the survivors of a single shipwreck, but Noah and his family survived a wreck of the world: "Every living substance was destroyed which was upon the face of the ground." Trembling with apprehension, yet grateful for safety, Noah built an altar unto the Lord and worshipped. The All Mighty and All Merciful accepted his offering and ratified his covenant by the rainbow (Iris), the Messiah of mythology. Is not the rainbow a fit illustration for "symbolic colours?" Is it not their source ? For the other illustrations I am indebted to my friend Mr. Field's philosophical works on colours. He has ably demonstrated their ratios ; yellow as the No. 3, red as 5, and blue as 8. Their combinations produce white and black by perfect absorption or reflection. Of this Essay he writes thus :—

"To render its ground more perspicuous we have prefixed a plate illustrating those first principles or elements of colours with which the work is in continual reference throughout. The Baron Portal adverts, in the commencement, to the dualism of *light* and *darkness* coeval with creation, which, being the types of colours, became in early history the symbols of the two principles of *benevolence* and *malevolence*, as recognised under every form of religion. He remarks, also, that the ancients admitted the two colours *black* and *white*, which are the two primitive elements of all other colours, and the ground of the analogy by which they are rendered symbolical; which also coincides with the demonstrations of philosophy, and justifies, to a considerable extent, the prevailing popular and poetical similitudes, and practical signification of colors."

"By the latent concurrence of light and shade, colours are generated or produced; and, as the various states of these principles are relative and convertible, we may deduce our proofs and examples from either. Thus, a *white spot upon a black ground*, or vice versâ, a black spot upon a white ground, viewed through a lensic prism, will be refracted into an aureola of the primary colours, as represented surrounding the spot, and in either case the *blue* will lie towards the passive or dark principle, and the *yellow* towards the active or light principle. Thus, colours, like figures, are generated in the simplest manner by the extension and expansion of a point in space; to which might be added many other coincidences.

"It is not necessary in this experiment that either of these principles should be in their absolute extreme, as black and white, or light and shade, it being sufficient that they should be relatively light and dark to afford this effect; nor is it necessary that they should not be coloured, since a spot of either of the foregoing colours, or of any hue, shade, or compound thereof, being formed upon a ground lighter or darker than itself, will also yield an aureola of the three primary colours, modified or ruled by its own particular hue."

"Thus the *primary colours* produced by analysis, or concurring in the synthesis of these principles or fundamentals in union, are *three :* the first and lowest number capable of uniting in variety, harmony, or system; and the variety of their union can be only three.

"An entire scale of colours is exhibited in the following engraving, as derived from these primaries in regular series from *white* to *black*, and relieved alternately by light and shade, and appears to be required for comparison, judgment, interpretation, and correction, of the analogous, moral, religious, natural, and technical symbolism throughout this interesting work; but if any reader wish further information concerning the more extensive relations and philosophy of colours founded on the above elements, he may derive satisfaction from Field's Chromatics, in which their relations and harmony are especially treated." *

* Works on Colours, &c., by George Field :—

CHROMATOGRAPHY, *or a Treatise on Colours and Pigments, and of their Powers in Painting;* including the Expression, Relations and Harmony, Physical Causes, Durability and Qualities of Colours and Pigments, individually and generally; with Illustrations, Descriptions, and Tables thereof. Also, an Account of the Vehicles, Varnishes, and Processes of Artists, Fresco Grounds, Picture Restoring, &c. A New Edition, Octavo.

DEFINITIVE SCALE OF COLOURS.

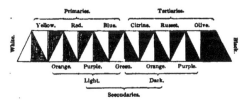

The primitive colours, and their secondary and tertiary combinations, are thus perceptible at a coup d'œil; yet the student may desire a more accurate definition of distinct colours: but there is some difficulty in affording it; they are so often evanescent, and dependent on the temperature and media through which they are viewed. Every spectator of a landscape may verify this remark; still there are appearances of colour whose nature is general and undeviating, viz.

White :—daylight; moonlight; the foam of the sea; the spray of the cataract; ice; snow; silver; milk; ivory; the lily.

Yellow :—gold; flame; the sun; the topaz; the primrose and other flowers.

Red :—blood; fire; the ruby; sunset.

Blue :—the firmament; the turquoise; the sapphire; lapis lazuli; ultramarine.

Black :—night; jet; coal; ebony.

In the undermentioned publications the connexion of colours with music, and the sciences of number and proportion; producing harmony and melody, is explained: not only fully confirming my brief notes of "Introduction" to this Essay, but also tending to rescue our old master, Vitruvius, from some imputations which a few modern schools have attempted to cast on him.

The translation is now submitted in the hope that a service will thus be rendered to our native school of architecture, by bringing to public notice these hitherto im-

CHROMATICS, or the Analogy, Harmony, and Philosophy of Colours; treating of the Principles of Colours and Colouring; their æsthetical relations with Forms, Sounds, and Signification throughout Art; the Chemical Doctrine of Vision, Light, and Colours, with Optical, Dioptrical, and Catoptrical Experiments, and Original Instruments. Illustrated by numerous Plates, Scales, and Coloured Diagrams. A New Edition, augmented, Octavo.

Former Edition of the same, with large Coloured Diagrams. Royal Quarto.

OUTLINES OF ANALOGICAL PHILOSOPHY. Being a primary view of the Principles, Relations, and Purposes of Nature, Science, and Art, in which the Sciences are digested, systematized, and harmonized with Nature and Art universally. 2 Volumes Octavo.

perfectly known illustrations of polychromy, the theory and practice of which, in the schools of France and Germany, have recently attracted much attention.

Few among the many studies essentially requisite to form the accomplished architect, require more delicate and accurate taste than the management of light and colours. Any decided opinion against the theories promulgated is deprecated until they have been æsthetically investigated, whereby principles of science and rules of art may be more truly evolved. Nor can the translator be responsible for allusions to religious emblems or analogies, some of which have been modified or omitted in deference to established opinions in this country.

It was my privilege, when a juvenile student, to hear the last lecture on colour, delivered in the Royal Academy, by the venerable President WEST. In subsequent years, when professionally engaged in directing extensive works for the supply of artificial light to some large cities, whilst discussing the illuminating power of various gases with the late eminent Professor Leslie, of Edinburgh, some curious properties of colour were incidentally mentioned. Occasional intervals of leisure have since enabled me to resume these studies, and if any of my professional brethren should derive similar pleasure, I shall be much gratified in having now alluded to them.

W. S. INMAN.

5, Kensington Upper Gore, Hyde Park,
   31st December, 1844.